Big Faith Little Religion, Little Faith Great Miracles

GODWIN BOOYSEN

Big Faith Little Religion, Little Faith Great Miracles

RETHINKING FAITH AND RELIGION

INSPiRED
PUBLISHING

Big Faith Little Religion, Little Faith Great Miracles
Rethinking Faith and Religion

First Edition, First Imprint 2025
ISBN: 978-1-83492-426-7
Copyright © Godwin Booysen

Editor: Eloise Scoble
Published by: Inspired Publishing
P O Box 82058 | Southdale | 2135 Johannesburg, RSA
Email: info@inspiredpublishing.co.za www.inspiredpublishing.co.za

DEDICATION

To my loving family - my wife Bukelwa and my daughters Faith, Omogolo, Kego — I dedicate this book. Your love, support, and encouragement have been my guiding light. Thank you for believing in me and my work. I look forward to sharing many more successes with you. The Best is yet to come!

CONTENTS

ACKNOWLEDGEMENTS

I would like to extend my heartfelt gratitude to Dr Christo Nel (Ds.) for his unwavering leadership and mentorship. His guidance has been instrumental in shaping my work, and I appreciate his constant encouragement to strive for excellence.

In memory of Dr Heyward Bruce Ewart III - Patriarch Paul, and Prof Marius Herholdt whose guidance and support were instrumental in shaping my worldview; both of them changed my life.

I also wish to express my special thanks to my colleagues who serve in the defence of our country. Their faith in my work and service has been a source of inspiration and motivation.

To Darren and the team at Inspired Publishing, I offer my sincerest appreciation. Your commitment to upholding high standards of values and professionalism is truly commendable, and it is evident that your work is making a positive impact in the world. Your dedication to changing lives is inspiring, and I am grateful for your contributions.

INTRODUCTION

What if the faith you grew up with isn't the faith you need now?

For many of us, faith was something we inherited. A tradition passed down. A set of rules we followed. But as life unfolds, and the questions get harder, we often find ourselves wrestling with what we were taught. The formulas stop working. The certainty slips through our fingers. And somewhere along the way, we begin to wonder—*Is there more?*

This book is for those who have dared to ask that question. For the ones who still believe, but not always in the way they used to. For the ones who love God, but aren't sure where they fit in anymore. It's not about abandoning what you knew. It's about holding space for what you're learning.

Big Faith isn't about performance. It's not about getting all the answers right. It's about rediscovering a faith that is bigger than fear, wider than religion, and deeper than doctrine. A faith that lives in questions just as much as it does in conviction. A faith that grows, stretches, breathes.

Let's begin by peeling back the layers. Before we can build something real, we need to be honest about where we've come from—and what might need to be rethought.

Rethinking Faith and Religion

We live in a world where faith and religion are often spoken of as if they are one and the same. They're used interchangeably in conversation, in books, and even from pulpits. Yet, when you pause and pay closer attention, it becomes clear—they are not identical. They're not even necessarily dependent on each other.

Faith is intimate. It's inward. It's that quiet trust, that stirring in your soul when all logic says to give up but something deeper whispers, "Hold on." It doesn't come in a neatly labelled package, and it often shows up without fanfare. Faith is what carries you when everything else falls away. It's the inner voice that reaches toward something greater than yourself—even when you don't have the words for it.

Religion, on the other hand, is more external. It's built. It's inherited. It often arrives with rituals, roles, and expectations. Religion gives structure to belief—offering sacred texts, shared practices, and communal identity. For some, this structure becomes a home. For others, it becomes a cage.

The poet Rabindranath Tagore once wrote, **"Faith is the bird that feels the light when the dawn is still dark."**[1] It's a beautiful image—one that reminds us that faith isn't always clear or visible. It moves before the sun rises. It senses light before it breaks. That kind of trust isn't taught by rules. It's born through experience—through moments that shake your certainty and still ask you to believe.

This book is about that kind of faith. Not the kind that must be proven, controlled, or defended. But the kind that finds you in the dark, walks with you through questions, and holds you even when you doubt everything.

Religion can be a powerful companion to faith. It can give faith a language. It can connect people across time and culture. It can shape values, deepen reverence, and provide a place to belong. But when religion becomes rigid—when it starts to dictate more than guide—it can lose its way. What was once a vessel for connection can become an obstacle to it.

Paul Tillich, the German-American theologian, captured this tension when he said, **"Religion is the organisation of spirituality, and spirituality is the personal experience of the sacred."** [2] In other words, religion is meant to hold the experience, not replace it. When we confuse the outer form for the inner fire, we risk losing the very thing we're seeking.

Many people have felt this tension—perhaps you have too. You may have grown up in a religious environment that gave you a strong moral compass, a sense of community, and deep traditions. But somewhere along the way, those same traditions might have begun to feel lifeless, like motions without meaning. Maybe your questions weren't welcomed. Maybe your story didn't fit neatly into the system. Maybe the rules mattered more than the relationship.

Others find faith not within religion, but beyond it. Outside the walls of a church or temple, faith can arise in nature, in art, in grief, in silence. It can emerge unexpectedly—often in the spaces where religion once failed. It's not a rebellion—it's a return. A return to something raw, authentic, and deeply human.

Deepak Chopra puts it this way: *"Faith is not the same as religion. Religion is a set of practices and beliefs, whereas faith is a state of being."* [3] That's an important distinction. Religion belongs to systems. Faith belongs to people. And people are messy, mysterious, and marvellously diverse. Faith, therefore, doesn't need to look the same for everyone. It lives in the heart, not in the handbook.

That doesn't mean religion has no value. When it reflects the beauty of the divine, when it protects the vulnerable, when it offers comfort and meaning—it becomes a sacred gift. But religion must serve faith, not the other way around.

This book is a journey. It's a conversation about what it means to hold faith without losing yourself to formality. It's about finding the courage to ask questions. To wrestle. To wonder. To seek a spirituality that makes room for honesty, emotion, and transformation.

Faith is not a checklist. It's not a badge or a title. It's not even a conclusion. It's a posture. An openness. A decision to lean into mystery. As Rainer Maria Rilke once wrote, *"Be patient toward all that is unsolved in your heart and try to love the questions themselves."*[4] To live by faith is to live with questions—not as enemies, but as companions.

You won't find formulas in these pages. But you will find reflections, wrestling's, and reimagining's. This is for the ones who have stayed, the ones who have left, and the ones who are still figuring it out. This is for those who want something more—something real.

Defining Faith and Religion

Faith Has Substance

We would be amiss to discuss faith and not unpack the biblical definition of Faith.

For all its mystery, faith is not vague. It's not wishful thinking or a soft cushion for hard times. Scripture doesn't leave us guessing.

The Bible gives us a definition of faith that's both powerful and gives us a language for what faith really is—not just how it feels, but what it *does*.

> *"Now faith is the substance of things hoped for, the evidence of things not seen."* – Hebrews 11:1 (KJV)

It's one of those verses that feels simple at first glance—but the more you sit with it, the deeper it goes. This isn't just a poetic line tucked away in Hebrews. It's a truth that has steadied hearts for generations.

Faith is not just a vague feeling or blind optimism. According to Scripture, it has *substance*. That word matters. It means faith isn't hollow.

In other words, it's real. Tangible. Weighty. Not because you can touch it with your hands, but because it holds things together on the inside. It is the *substance* of things hoped for—meaning, faith gives shape to our hope. It's what allows hope to stand, even before the outcome arrives. It's not a placeholder until something more "concrete" shows up.

Think of it like this: Hope looks ahead. Faith holds hope in place. Hope dreams. Faith builds a foundation under that dream, even when everything around you still looks the same.

The verse goes on: faith is also *the evidence of things not seen.* That's the mystery. Faith isn't proved by sight—it *is* the proof. It's what keeps you steady when nothing else adds up. It's the inner conviction that says, *"God is still working, even when I can't see it yet."*

Faith doesn't ignore reality. It just refuses to be limited by it. It sees beyond what's visible and leans into what is eternal. It believes that the invisible realm—where God is always moving—is just as real as what we can see or measure.

This kind of faith doesn't come from having all the answers. It comes from knowing Who holds them.

It is steady. It is sure. And it gives us something to stand on when everything else feels uncertain.

It is steady.
It is sure.
And it gives us something to stand on when everything else feels uncertain.

But here's the beautiful thing: for all its substance, faith is also deeply poetic. It carries weight, yes—but it also carries wonder. It's both anchor and ache. It builds a foundation, but it also reaches beyond what's seen, stretching into mystery.

And that's where we begin to sense its other side—the side that isn't defined by doctrine or structure, but by something more intuitive. Something more tender. Because faith isn't only about holding ground. Sometimes, it's about sensing light you can't yet see.

That's why, as Deepak Chopra puts it, *"Faith is not a rational conclusion, but an intuitive leap."* [5]

To better understand why faith and religion aren't the same, we need to look closely at how they're shaped—and how they shape us.

Faith is deeply personal. It doesn't start with a sermon or a tradition. It starts with an ache, a longing, a hope. It may begin in joy, or it may be born out of grief. Either way, it grows quietly, like a seed pushed into the dark soil of our lives. Faith isn't something you recite—it's something you live. And often, it doesn't arrive fully formed. It develops over time, shaped by life, tested by disappointment, and strengthened in moments of surrender.

Faith connects us to something bigger than ourselves—whether we call that God, Spirit, the Divine, or simply love. It's a sense that there's more to life than what we see. More than just logic. More than just routine. Faith is where trust lives when the facts don't make sense. It's what gives meaning to mystery.

Religion, in contrast, is the structure we often build around faith. It's the container. Religion offers belief systems, sacred texts, traditions, and rituals. It helps communities organise their spiritual expressions. It gives language to the unseen and rhythm to the sacred. Religion can be rich in symbolism, beautiful in practice, and deeply comforting in its continuity. It creates connection—both to God and to others.

But religion can also become rigid. When it stops evolving, it starts enforcing. When it stops serving people, it starts controlling them. At its best, religion helps faith take shape. At its worst, it replaces faith altogether. What was once a path becomes a wall.

As Thomas Merton once wrote, *"The beginning of love is the will to let those we love be perfectly themselves."* [6] That same grace applies to faith—it must be free to grow, to stretch, to become. When we box it in too tightly with rules and rigidity, we don't protect it—we silence it.

Deepak Chopra helps clarify this further: "Religion is a set of practices and beliefs. Faith is a state of being." [7] Religion can be followed. Faith must be felt. Religion can be taught. Faith must be experienced. You can join a religion. But faith—you have to live that yourself.

The difference matters. Because how we define these things shapes how we relate to them—and how we relate to ourselves.

Key Differences

So what exactly separates faith from religion?

Let's begin with orientation.

Faith turns inward. It's personal. Private. Emotional. It begins inside the heart, not inside a system. It may be shaped by tradition, but it isn't defined by it. Faith is like a compass—it helps you navigate your own spiritual path. Sometimes it leads you into the wild. Sometimes into the quiet. It doesn't always make sense on paper, but it carries you anyway.

Religion, on the other hand, turns outward. It's communal. Public. Organised. Religion builds structures to help express faith collectively. It codifies beliefs and outlines practices. It offers a shared language for the sacred. But in doing so, it can also become a checklist—a system to maintain, rather than a mystery to live.

Then there's the matter of experience.

Faith is subjective. It's tied to your own story, your wounds, and your wonder. It might not be easy to explain, but you know it when you feel it. It grows with you. It shifts with you. It challenges you—and it carries you through the hardest seasons.

Religion is more objective. It relies on teachings, doctrines, liturgies, and traditions passed down over generations. These can be beautiful and powerful—but they're not always personal. They're shared, communal, and often unchanged over time. That stability can feel like comfort, or it can feel like confinement.

Finally, we see the difference in the question of motivation.

Faith longs for connection. It wants to draw near to the sacred. It's about presence, intimacy, surrender. Faith says, "I want to know You." It's not about getting everything right—it's about staying open, even when things go wrong.

Religion, if unchecked, can demand compliance. It can prioritise conformity, outward appearances, and strict observance of rules. In trying to preserve something sacred, it can lose its soul. It can leave people feeling judged instead of embraced. Pressured instead of pursued.

Still, this isn't about throwing religion away. It's about returning it to its proper place—as a servant of faith, not a substitute for it. When religion supports our faith rather than suffocates it, it becomes something beautiful: a vessel for belonging, a home for our searching, and a language for the sacred.

But when religion forgets its purpose—when it becomes about fear, performance, or power—it no longer carries life. It merely imitates it.

Faith is not against religion. But it must remain free from being owned by it.

PART I

BIG FAITH LITTLE RELIGION

CHAPTER 1

THE CONVENTIONAL RELIGIOUS BELIEVER: A CRITIQUE OF UNEXAMINED FAITH

Not all belief is the same.

Some people inherit their beliefs the way you might inherit an old coat—passed down, worn in, but never questioned. It fits well enough, and so it's worn without thinking. For many, this is what faith becomes: something received, not something wrestled with.

The philosopher William James described this well over a century ago. He said, *"I speak now not of your ordinary religious believer, who follows the conventional observances of his country, whether it be Buddhist, Christian, or Mohammedan. His religion has been made for him by others, communicated to him by tradition, determined by fixed forms of imitation and retained by habit."*[8]

James wasn't mocking believers—he was naming a common pattern. Many people are born into systems that define their beliefs before they've even had the chance to ask real questions. And often, those questions are discouraged. In such systems, faith becomes memorised rather than realised. Obedience is rewarded. Doubt is silenced. And the substance of belief becomes secondary to the structure that holds it.

This kind of faith is not necessarily false—but it is fragile. It doesn't grow roots because it hasn't wrestled with the real world. It hasn't been tested in pain or reshaped through personal experience. And when crisis comes—and it always does—this borrowed belief can unravel quickly.

Authentic faith cannot be handed to you. It must be discovered, nurtured, and lived. That doesn't mean rejecting tradition or turning your back on your roots. It means being willing to examine what you've been taught, to question what no longer fits, and to pursue a connection with the divine that is truly your own.

The journey from unexamined religion to awakened faith is not a rejection—it's a return. A return to sincerity. To encounter. To real spiritual agency.

The Need for Rethinking: Challenging Conventional Narratives
Traditional religion has shaped cultures, families, and civilisations. It has carried wisdom, preserved truth, and brought comfort to countless lives. But it has also, in many cases, become too rigid. Too narrow. Too focused on control and compliance, rather than transformation and connection.

When religion becomes more about fear than faith, more about rules than relationship, it starts to lose its power to heal. Instead of lifting people up, it weighs them down. Instead of freeing the soul, it binds it with guilt, shame, and anxiety.

It's time to pause and ask some honest questions:

Is the way we've been taught to believe still serving our growth? Does our expression of religion still open the heart—or does it close it? Are we clinging to systems that no longer reflect the God we know deep down?

Challenging these inherited systems is not about dishonouring the past. It's about honouring the truth. Faith, after all, is alive. And living things grow. They stretch. They shed old skin. They adapt to new seasons.

To rethink religion is not to reject it. It's to make space for a more expansive, compassionate, and honest spirituality. A kind of faith that doesn't ask us to silence our doubts, but welcomes them. A faith that doesn't shrink when challenged, but deepens. A faith that doesn't demand performance, but invites presence.

As Carl Jung once said, *"The greatest sin is unconsciousness."*[9] When we simply go through the motions of belief without ever truly waking up, we miss the whole point. Faith is not about sleepwalking through rituals—it's about coming alive.

This rethinking begins with courage—the courage to examine long-held beliefs, to hold space for questions, and to trust that what is real and sacred can withstand scrutiny.

When we do that, something shifts. The walls start to fall. The fear begins to fade. And in its place, a deeper kind of faith emerges—one rooted not in tradition alone, but in truth, love, and lived experience.

The Limitations of Traditional Views

Traditional views of faith and religion can be limiting or even harmful in several ways:

Dogmatic Thinking: The Enemy of Faith and Personal Growth

Not all religion is harmful. But when it becomes rigid—when it no longer reflects the movement of the Spirit or the reality of human experience—it can cause real harm.

For many, traditional religious teachings have provided safety, meaning, and a moral compass. But for others, these same teachings have become heavy with shame, restrictive in expression, and resistant to change. Instead of leading people into deeper faith, they lead people into disillusionment.

We need to name these limitations. Not to condemn religion, but to free it. To make space for something more honest, more expansive, more alive.

1. **Dogmatic Thinking: When Mystery Is Replaced by Control**
   One of the most serious challenges within traditional religion is dogma. Dogma is the insistence that a particular set of beliefs is absolute, unchangeable, and beyond question. It closes the door to exploration. It makes doubt a threat, and mystery an enemy.

But true faith was never meant to be boxed in. It grows best in the soil of curiosity. It flourishes when it's allowed to breathe.

Theologian Paul Tillich warned, *"Dogma is the enemy of faith, because it tries to fix the mystery of God."* [10] When we try to nail down every detail of the divine, we reduce God to a formula. But God is not a system. God is spirit, breath, wind—uncontainable.

Faith is not about having all the answers. It's about learning to trust in the absence of answers. But dogmatic systems demand certainty. And when people are taught that their worth depends on getting it all "right," faith stops being a source of freedom and becomes a source of fear.

2. **Fear and Guilt: Controlling the Heart Instead of Freeing It**
   One of the most damaging legacies of certain religious systems is the use of fear and guilt to govern people's inner lives. Rather than awakening love, such systems enforce obedience by threatening divine punishment or shame. The result is often a spirituality driven not by relationship, but by fear of rejection.

When the core message of faith is distorted into fear of failure or punishment, the heart begins to close. People no longer approach God with freedom and trust—they approach with dread. This can hollow out the soul of a person who genuinely longs for truth but feels forever unworthy to receive it.

A more nourishing perspective is offered by Brené Brown, who writes, ***"Shame corrodes the very part of us that believes we are capable of change."*** [11] In environments where guilt and shame are the tools of control, transformation becomes nearly impossible. The soul doesn't bloom under pressure—it shrinks.

Real faith invites responsibility, not paralysis. It calls us to face ourselves with honesty, but never with hatred. True spiritual growth comes not from guilt, but from grace. From knowing we are seen fully—and still loved. When we remove fear from the equation, the heart is finally free to open, to heal, and to grow.

3. **Exclusivity and Division: The Problem of "Us vs Them"**
   Another common issue within traditional religion is exclusivity—
   the belief that only a select few are chosen, saved, or right.

This creates barriers. It divides people. It makes room for pride and prejudice, often under the guise of spiritual authority. Instead of unity, we get separation. Instead of shared humanity, we get suspicion.

Doctrinal walls may protect a community's identity, but they can also prevent that community from loving others freely. And when religion becomes more concerned with who's "in" and who's "out," it stops reflecting the heart of God.

Eckhart Tolle once said, *"The primary cause of unhappiness is never the situation but rather your thoughts about it."* [12] So often, our unhappiness isn't caused by others—but by the ways we've been taught to see them. When religion tells us who to fear or exclude, it robs us of the joy of connection.

But there is another way. A way of compassion. A way of welcome. A way of recognising that every person is created in the image of God, whether or not they look, speak, or worship the same as we do.

4. **The Need for a Fresh Perspective**
   None of this is new. People have been questioning tradition for centuries. The prophets challenged the temple systems. Jesus pushed against the religious norms of His day. Reformers throughout history have spoken up when faith lost its way.

We stand in that same moment now.

If our religion no longer opens us to love, if it no longer makes room for wonder, if it no longer allows people to grow—then we must return to the beginning. Not to destroy, but to rebuild. Not to abandon, but to reawaken.

A fresh perspective doesn't mean throwing everything out. It means asking: What is still life-giving? What is still true? And what must evolve so that our faith can breathe again?

This is not an easy path. It asks for courage. For unlearning. For humility. But it also invites transformation—the kind that doesn't come from rules or rituals, but from real, honest encounter with the Divine.

A Fresh Perspective: Growing Beyond the Old

It's not enough to name what no longer works—we must also imagine what's possible.

If traditional religion has, at times, limited or harmed us, what does a freer, fuller faith look like?

A faith that welcomes questions.
A faith that doesn't fear mystery.
A faith that awakens both the mind and the heart.
A faith that builds bridges instead of walls.

That kind of faith begins with three powerful shifts: Embracing uncertainty, fostering critical thinking, and cultivating compassion.

1. **Embracing Uncertainty: Making Peace with the Unknown**
   So much of religion has been built on certainty—on knowing who God is, what God wants, and how the world works. But life rarely fits that neatly. And neither does faith.

True faith is not about clinging to answers—it's about learning to live inside the questions.

Richard Feynman, a Nobel Prize-winning physicist, once said, *"I think I can safely say that nobody understands quantum mechanics."* [13] If even the finest minds admit their limits in science, how much more should we admit our limits when it comes to the divine?

Faith is not a system to master. It's a mystery to enter. The unknown isn't a threat—it's an invitation. It draws us deeper. It softens us. It teaches us to trust in what we can't yet see.

When we embrace uncertainty, we don't lose faith—we strengthen it. Because now it's not rooted in having control, but in surrendering to something bigger.

Uncertainty becomes sacred ground—the place where awe returns and humility grows.

2. **Fostering Critical Thinking: Faith That Asks Questions**
    Faith is not blind. It doesn't require you to shut off your mind or ignore your instincts. In fact, real faith invites you to think more deeply, not less.

Socrates said, *"The unexamined life is not worth living."* [14] That's true of faith as well. If we never stop to ask why we believe what we believe, we risk building our lives on someone else's foundation.

Critical thinking is not the enemy of belief—it's the path to deeper belief. When we question, we aren't being rebellious; we're being honest. We're seeking a faith that fits, not just one that's handed down.

This means letting go of the fear that questioning will lead us away from God. Often, it leads us straight to Him—but without the noise. Without the masks. Without the fear of being struck down for wondering.

God is not afraid of your questions. He gave you the mind to ask them.

3. **Cultivating Inclusivity and Compassion: Returning to Love**
    Finally, any fresh perspective on faith must lead us back to compassion.

What good is belief if it makes us bitter? What good is being "right" if it makes us cruel?

Ram Dass once said, *"We're all just walking each other home."* [15] That one line says everything.

We're not here to conquer each other. We're not here to divide the world into worthy and unworthy. We're here to love. To listen. To carry each other when we fall.

True faith will always lead us to mercy. It will always soften our eyes. It will always remind us that no matter our differences, we are still human. Still beloved. Still neighbours.

When compassion becomes the centre of our spirituality, something shifts. We stop trying to win arguments and start trying to heal hearts. We stop drawing lines and start extending hands. We stop fearing strangers and start recognising family.

These three shifts—uncertainty, critical thought, and compassion—do not make our faith weaker. They make it real.

This is the beginning of something new.
Not a rebellion.
Not a rejection.
But a return.

A return to what faith was always meant to be:
Alive.
Honest.
Transformative.

Personal Story:

My own journey shows just how important it is to rethink faith and religion, and how powerful it can be to embrace a more open and inclusive approach to spirituality.

I was fortunate to grow up around people who lived with integrity and strong values, though I hesitate to say I was raised in a traditional Christian household. Some of my earliest memories of spiritual life go back to before I even started school—walking with my grandmother through our village to attend church. I don't remember much about the services themselves, but looking back, I believe those moments planted early seeds in my spiritual journey.

Between the ages of 12 and 16, I drifted away from the Church and found myself questioning everything—God's existence, the authority and validity of the Bible, and the-core beliefs of Christianity. Living in South Africa, I was exposed to the harsh realities of exploitation and inequality. It was hard to accept the religious ideas that, to me, seemed to justify or ignore these injustices. At school, our teachers would elaborate on the dark history of African people groups, and the suffering endured by them. I struggled to reconcile that history and those atrocities with the idea of a just and loving God.

But everything changed when I was sixteen. On Easter Sunday of 1989, something shifted inside me. I responded to the message with tears and trembling. I felt a clear, powerful and unmistakable calling to serve in ministry within the Methodist Church. My dream was to attend a seminary after high school, but I was also drawn to the military. In the end, I chose the military path.

During that time, I joined the Young Men's Guild, and outside the walls of the Methodist Church, I encountered Pentecostal street preachers whose message resonated with me. Their boldness, their passion—it spoke to something in me. I began to take on their preaching style and by 1993, during my early years in the military, I started leading church services for fellow soldiers when no chaplain was available.

This continued until 1997— even after chaplains were assigned to our unit. Eventually, I felt such a strong sense of calling and purpose that I decided to leave the military and establish an independent ministry. But ten months later, I was reappointed —this time, officially—as a Chaplain. A role I've now served in for the past 27 years.

Throughout my journey, I've had the privilege of serving in various military units while also running a parallel church ministry for ten years. I've officiated weddings, spoken at graduations, and offered comfort to widows and families of fallen soldiers. I've been decorated for my service and have had the honour of addressing government ministers and military generals.

Over the past two decades, I've experienced significant personal growth and transformation, alongside many milestones. This journey has not only been incredibly fulfilling but has also shaped and deepened my understanding of faith and spirituality in powerful ways.

My spiritual exploration has taken me through several Christian denominations, including Methodist, Pentecostal Holiness, Evangelical, and Anglo-Catholic traditions. Within some of these denominations, I've held senior leadership roles, which have taught me much and widened my spiritual perspective. These varied experiences have collectively helped to shape and enrich my faith in ways I never expected. It is this evolution that I invite you to explore with me in this book.

The Problem with Traditional Religion

There's no denying the impact of religion across centuries. It has built communities, inspired revolutions, and shaped cultures. But at the same time, traditional religion—when left unexamined—can do real damage.

It can hold people back instead of setting them free. It can create fear instead of wonder. It can reduce spirituality to performance, rather than allowing it to be a place of deep personal encounter.

This isn't about dishonouring the past. It's about looking honestly at where things have become misaligned, and where the call of Jesus—to love, to liberate, to transform—has been muffled under layers of doctrine and tradition.

Let's explore three areas where traditional religion often falls short: dogma, judgment, and disconnection.

1. **When Doctrine Becomes a Cage**
    Every belief system needs structure. But when those structures become immovable, they stop serving people. They start controlling them.

Dogma says, "This is the only way. Don't ask questions. Don't think too hard. Don't challenge the system." It values certainty over growth, control over conversation.

As Christian mystic Richard Rohr puts it, ***"The opposite of faith is not doubt, but control."*** [1] Faith thrives in the unknown. But when religion turns the mystery of God into a formula, it stops pointing us toward wonder and starts demanding compliance.

History gives us plenty of examples. Galileo was condemned by the Church for daring to suggest that the earth revolved around the sun. Why? Because it threatened religious power structures. And while science eventually caught up, the deeper issue remains—when religious institutions fear being wrong, they silence anyone who asks different questions.

But faith was never meant to be a fixed set of answers. It was meant to be a living relationship. Something that grows, changes, and deepens over time. When religion becomes obsessed with protecting its doctrine, it often forgets its people.

2. **When Judgement Replaces Grace**
   One of the most painful things about traditional religion is the way it often divides people. It draws lines between the holy and the unholy, the saved and the lost, the worthy and the fallen.

This judgement can be subtle—a sideways glance at someone different—or it can be overt, enforced through sermons, policies, or silence. Either way, the result is the same: shame, isolation, and fear.

Psychologist Carl Rogers once said, *"The most damaging aspect of traditional religion is its tendency to create a sense of guilt and shame in individuals."* [2] When spirituality is used to make people feel smaller, it ceases to be spiritual at all.

God does not operate through shame. Jesus didn't withhold love from those who didn't fit. He touched lepers. He dined with outcasts. He spoke to women others ignored. If our faith leads us to judge more than it leads us to love, it's no longer shaped by the Gospel.

We must be willing to confront the ways religion has become a weapon instead of a shelter. And we must return to grace—not as a doctrine, but as a way of being.

3. When Rituals Lose Their Meaning

Rituals are meant to connect us to something sacred. But when they become hollow, they can leave us feeling more disconnected than ever.

Traditional religion often emphasises rules, rites, and formal observances. These can be meaningful when done with intention—but over time, they can become routine. Something you do to check a box, not to connect with God.

You attend services, say the prayers, sing the hymns—but something still feels missing. You go through the motions, but your soul stays silent.

Thomas Merton once wrote, *"The danger of education, I have found, is that it so easily confuses means with ends."* [3] That same danger applies to religion. The structure is meant to serve the Spirit—not replace it. When rituals become ends in themselves, they risk becoming spiritual noise instead of nourishment.

And when we're taught that questioning these practices is dangerous, we end up stuck. We suppress our own longings. We doubt our own hearts. We live out someone else's spirituality instead of discovering our own.

But faith was never meant to be sterile. It was never meant to be cold. God is not moved by how well we perform rituals. God meets us in honesty, in longing, in real relationship.

So what happens when we've outgrown these systems?

What do we do when the faith that once held us now feels too small, too scripted, too far from who we're becoming?

We begin again.

Not with rebellion, but with return.

Not with shame, but with freedom.

Not with noise, but with a whisper:

There's more. There has always been more.

CHAPTER 2

THE POWER OF BIG FAITH, LITTLE RELIGION: REDEFINING FAITH FOR A NEW ERA

In a time where many are walking away from religion but still yearning for something sacred, the concept of **Big Faith** Little Religion offers a timely and liberating alternative. It calls us back to the heart of spirituality—away from rigid systems and towards a living, breathing connection with the divine. Big Faith Little Religion invites us to prioritise personal relationship, compassion, and growth over external forms, traditions, or theological correctness.

At its core, Big Faith is deeply personal. It doesn't ask for blind belief in a set of doctrines. It asks for sincerity. For authenticity. It recognises that true faith can't be reduced to formulas, rituals, or creeds—it must be lived, wrestled with, and experienced firsthand. Whether you name the divine as God, Spirit, Source, or simply Mystery, Big Faith Little Religion makes room for that sacred relationship to unfold uniquely in each life.

Where traditional religion has often emphasised uniformity, Big Faith Little Religion honours diversity. It understands that spiritual journeys are not linear, and that people arrive at truth through different doors. Rather than dividing people into insiders and outsiders, it invites all to the table. It holds space for both certainty and doubt, for tradition and questioning, for reverence and reimagining. Big Faith Little Religion doesn't fear difference—it celebrates it.

This approach does not reject the Church, Scripture, or community. Instead, it reorders their place. Big Faith values these things as tools, not as gatekeepers. It sees spiritual authority not as something imposed from above, but as something discovered within. It encourages us to take ownership of our faith, to listen to the still small voice, and to seek connection rather than control.

By embracing Big Faith Little Religion, we free ourselves from the need to perform or pretend. We become open to wonder again. We ask questions, engage with others honestly, and build a spiritual life that reflects who we are and what we're becoming. It's faith that evolves, that breathes, and that grows with us.

Ultimately, Big Faith doesn't just shape what we believe—it transforms how we live. It teaches us to love wider, to hold others more gently, and to walk humbly with mystery. In a world fractured by religious division and spiritual exhaustion, Big Faith offers a path back to wholeness—a way to rediscover the sacred in the everyday, and the divine within us all.

Key Principles of Big Faith

1. **Personal Connection: Cultivating a Personal, Experiential Relationship with the Divine**

   At the heart of **Big Faith** is personal connection—a deep, experiential relationship with the divine that cannot be mediated by dogma, doctrine, or institutional authority. This principle affirms that true spirituality begins with an inward encounter. As theologian Paul Tillich said, *"Faith is the state of being ultimately concerned."* [1] This speaks to a faith that isn't about compliance, but about connection—a sacred concern that draws us into communion with something greater than ourselves.

This connection is intimate and unique. It doesn't follow a single formula or require a specific religious label. It emerges in the quiet moments, in honest questions, in the soul's longing to know and be known. It becomes a compass, anchoring us in meaning and direction. When faith is lived from this place, it no longer feels like duty—it feels like home.

Big Faith invites us to move beyond borrowed beliefs into something lived and real. It doesn't demand we abandon tradition, but it does ask that we go deeper than routine. It recognises that many people have felt spiritually disconnected not because they lacked belief, but because they lacked experience—because their spiritual life was confined to rituals, creeds, or institutions that never truly met them where they were.

Unlike traditional religion, which often places intermediaries between the individual and the divine, Big Faith insists that every person can access God directly. This direct connection doesn't need to be explained or justified. It simply needs to be nurtured.

Whether you come from a Christian, Muslim, Buddhist, or entirely different background, this principle applies. Big Faith affirms that the divine is not owned by any single system—it is present and available to all. Across every culture and spiritual path, the desire for connection is a universal cry of the soul.

In contrast, when faith is reduced to memorising creeds or conforming to institutional expectations, people can become disconnected from their own experiences, emotions, and inner wisdom. Big Faith reclaims this inner life. It encourages us to trust what we know deeply, to follow the stirrings of the Spirit, and to build a faith that is both personal and transformative.

1.1 Inclusivity: Embracing Diversity and Promoting a Sense of Shared Humanity

Another cornerstone of **Big Faith** is *inclusivity*—the courageous and wholehearted embrace of diversity in all its forms. Big Faith does not seek to erase difference, but to honour it. It welcomes a broad spectrum of spiritual expressions, perspectives, and questions, recognising that there is no single path to the divine, and no one spiritual experience that encompasses them all.

As Deepak Chopra notes, *"Spirituality is the experience of that which is beyond the confines of the physical body and the limitations of the mind."*[2] This reminder invites us to move past the narrow boundaries of doctrine and into the vastness of shared spiritual experience. It invites us to see others not as theological opponents, but as fellow seekers.

Inclusivity, in the context of Big Faith, is more than tolerance—it is celebration. It is the intentional choice to see beauty in what is different, and to remain open to what we do not yet understand. It creates space for people to show up fully—as they are—without fear of exclusion or shame. Whether someone grew up in a strict religious environment, follows a different tradition, or is just beginning their spiritual exploration, they are welcomed without condition.

Traditional religion has often operated with an insider–outsider framework, drawing lines around who belongs and who doesn't. This has led to fragmentation—people divided not only by belief, but by judgment and suspicion. Big Faith seeks to heal that divide. It holds the door open. It believes that spirituality, at its truest, brings us together rather than pulling us apart. When we practise this kind of inclusivity, we begin to rediscover our shared humanity. We listen better. We hold space more generously. And in doing so, we reflect the nature of the divine—who is not limited by creed or culture, but who speaks to the soul of every person in a language they can understand.

Big Faith creates communities marked not by sameness, but by belonging. It affirms that you don't have to believe the same things to walk the same path. You just have to walk in love.

2. **Compassion: The Heart of Big Faith**

   Compassion stands at the very centre of Big Faith. More than an emotion, it is a deliberate posture of the heart—a lived expression of empathy, kindness, and shared humanity. In a world often marked by division and difference, compassion invites us to remember what unites us. As the Dalai Lama notes, "*Compassion is not just a feeling, but a choice.*" (Dalai Lama, 1999) [3] It is a conscious decision to treat others with dignity, patience, and grace.

   This principle encourages individuals to move beyond sentiment into action. Compassion asks us to slow down, to listen with openness, and to acknowledge the struggles and stories that shape others' lives. It recognises that while our beliefs and backgrounds may differ, we are each navigating pain, joy, longing, and love. Big Faith honours this shared experience and insists that true spirituality cannot be separated from how we treat one another.

Whereas traditional religious institutions have sometimes placed doctrine above people, Big Faith insists that compassion is itself a form of theology. It's the lived theology of mercy, of inclusion, of presence. When compassion is centred, we begin to experience God not only in sacred texts or rituals, but also in how we show up for the hurting, the misunderstood, and the overlooked.

This kind of compassion doesn't dilute conviction—it deepens it. It reminds us that our faith is not proven in how right we are, but in how well we love. By placing compassion at the heart of spiritual practice, Big Faith invites us to live our beliefs with warmth, integrity, and grace.

3. **Growth: The Lifelong Journey of Spiritual Evolution**

   Growth is a foundational principle of Big Faith. It calls us to embrace spirituality not as a fixed set of beliefs, but as a living, breathing journey—one marked by reflection, learning, and transformation. As Carl Jung observed, *"The journey of self-discovery is a lifelong process."* (Jung, 1964) [4] Big Faith honours this process, encouraging individuals to remain open, curious, and willing to evolve.

   Where traditional religion can sometimes equate faithfulness with staying the same, Big Faith recognises that true spiritual maturity often involves change. It allows room for questions. It makes space for seasons of doubt and discovery. It understands that beliefs can deepen, shift, and expand as we encounter new truths, experiences, and insights. Spiritual growth is not a betrayal of tradition—it is a sign of life. When we stop evolving, we risk spiritual stagnation, where faith becomes performative or disconnected from our lived experience. Big Faith resists this by nurturing a spirituality that moves with us, not against us. This kind of growth doesn't just change how we see God—it changes how we see ourselves and others. It helps us shed the false layers imposed by fear or rigidity and invites us to become more whole, more present, and more grounded in love.

By choosing growth, we commit to a lifelong unfolding. We learn to walk in humility, to welcome wisdom from unexpected places, and to trust that spiritual depth is found not in arriving, but in the willingness to keep going. "None of us is an arriver. We're all pilgrims and becomers." Doug Murren (1999)

Embracing Paradox: The Liberating Power of "Big Faith Little Religion"

At first glance, the phrases *Big Faith Little Religion* may seem to contradict one another. Big Faith suggests a broad, inclusive, and ever-expanding view of spirituality. Little Religion, by contrast, hints at something pared back—personal, minimal, and unconcerned with institutional structure. But it is precisely in this tension that a liberating paradox emerges. When held together, these ideas reveal a pathway to deeper, more authentic faith. Big Faith calls us to trust in something vast and mysterious, something greater than ourselves. It invites awe, wonder, and connection. Little Religion, on the other hand, invites us to hold that faith lightly—without the weight of rigid dogma or institutional control. It says you don't need to have all the answers, follow every rule, or belong to a certain group in order to experience the sacred.

By letting go of the need for religious certainty or conformity, we make room for a more personal, dynamic relationship with the divine. Free from the fear of judgement or the pressure to perform, our spiritual lives become more honest—shaped by real encounters, sincere questions, and meaningful exploration. In this space, faith is not imposed—it is discovered.

41

Little Religion also guards us from the traps of spiritual elitism. When we believe that only certain people have access to truth or belonging, we create barriers rather than bridges. But Big Faith reminds us that God is not confined to one tradition, language, or practice. It reclaims mystery, celebrates difference, and honours every person's sacred path. Rather than creating tension, this paradox offers harmony. Big Faith gives us vision. Little Religion gives us freedom. Together, they make faith both transcendent and tangible—grounded in experience, yet open to the infinite. It is in this balance that many find their most honest and life-giving spirituality.

The Paradox of Big Faith Little Religion: Embracing Freedom and Autonomy

The phrase *Big Faith Little Religion* captures a paradox—yet within it lies a deeply liberating approach to spiritual life. Rather than rejecting faith altogether, it invites us to embrace belief with open hands and clear eyes. It proposes that a rich, expansive faith can actually thrive when unburdened by the heavy layers of religious dogma and institutional control.

"You do not need to know precisely what is happening, or exactly where it is all going. What you need is to recognise the possibilities and challenges offered by the present moment, and to embrace them with courage, faith, and hope." – Thomas Merton (Merton, 1961) [1]

This kind of trust does not need to be filtered through rigid systems or enforced conformity. In fact, it's often when we move away from those structures that we begin to develop an authentic, lived relationship with the divine. *Little Religion* allows room for honesty. It gives permission to question, to search, and to grow.

This freedom is not a dismissal of all tradition—it's a reorientation. It's about choosing autonomy over obligation. Psychologist Abraham Maslow observed that *"the most effective way to develop autonomy is to take responsibility for one's own life."* (Maslow, 1962) [2] That same principle applies spiritually. When we step into ownership of our journey, rather than outsourcing it to a system, our faith becomes personal, alive, and rooted in lived experience. Autonomy in faith does not mean isolation. On the contrary, those who walk this path often find themselves more deeply connected to others—not through shared doctrine, but through shared humanity. Freed from religious gatekeeping, we can relate with compassion rather than comparison, presence rather than performance.

Traditional religion has often emphasised obedience over ownership. But this can lead to passivity, spiritual detachment, or a reliance on external approval. *Big Faith Little Religion* offers a way out of that cycle. It empowers individuals to grow, evolve, and respond to God directly—without needing permission.

In this paradox, freedom and reverence walk together. Faith becomes something we carry within, not something enforced from without. And that kind of faith—chosen freely, nurtured intentionally—can lead to the most profound transformation of all.

Great Miracles

When we combine *Big Faith* with *Little Religion*, something powerful happens. Lives change. Hearts heal. People rise. This blend creates space for great miracles—not just in the spiritual sense, but in the practical, everyday outworking of our lives. It opens the door for growth, impact, and real transformation.

The Potential of Big Faith Little Religion: Unlocking Growth and Lasting Change

When we step into *Big Faith* without the weight of rigid religion, we begin to grow in new ways. That growth isn't forced or shallow—it's rooted, steady, and real. It's the kind that brings us home to ourselves, while drawing us deeper into relationship with God.

As theologian Frederick Buechner put it, *"Listen to your life. See it for the fathomless mystery that it is. In the boredom and pain of it no less than in the excitement and gladness: touch, taste, smell your way to the holy and hidden heart of it."* (Buechner, 1992) [3] This kind of faith invites us into that mystery—a lifelong unfolding, full of learning and becoming.

This kind of faith also brings purpose. It opens our eyes to the needs around us and gives us the courage to do something about them. It softens our hearts and strengthens our hands. As the Dalai Lama reminds us, *"Compassion is not just a feeling, but a choice."* (Dalai Lama, 1999) [4] When we choose compassion, we begin to live out our faith in ways that matter—in our homes, our communities, and the world beyond us.

Big Faith Little Religion also helps us access new wells of clarity, creativity, and strength. In a world full of noise, it draws us back to stillness. It reminds us that some of the greatest breakthroughs come not through striving, but through quiet trust. As Eckhart Tolle writes, *"True intelligence operates silently. Stillness is where creativity and solutions to problems are found."* [5]

It's in that stillness that faith takes root and grows strong. Traditional religion can sometimes limit that growth—placing emphasis on performance, perfection, or external rules. But when we make room for a deeper kind of faith, we begin to live with courage and conviction.

We become more grounded, more open, and more in tune with what really matters.

This is the invitation of *Big Faith Little Religion*—to live fully, love deeply, and believe boldly. Not because we have to, but because we were made for it.

Understanding Big Faith

1. Defining Big Faith: Beyond Traditional Notions

Big Faith is a bold and freeing way of looking at spirituality. It moves beyond the usual expectations of religion and opens the door to something more personal, more human, and more connected. At its heart, Big Faith recognises that spiritual life isn't just about attending a service or following a set of rules—it's about the journey of the soul, the questions we ask, and the connection we feel.

Unlike traditional frameworks that often rely on doctrine, hierarchy, and rigid belief systems, Big Faith places value on your personal experience—your intuition, your wrestle, and your wonder. It acknowledges that there isn't just one way to approach God or live out your faith. People grow in different ways, in different seasons, and faith must have room for that. Henri Nouwen reminds us, *"The spiritual life does not remove us from the world but leads us deeper into it."* *(Nouwen, 1975) [1]* This deepening—this drawing in—is something we all long for, regardless of our background or label.

Big Faith sees spirituality as something that belongs to everyone, regardless of religion, culture, or tradition. It isn't about fitting into a box. It's about growing into the fullness of who you are. Carl Jung described the journey of the soul as a lifelong process of discovery and unfolding [2] Big Faith makes space for that kind of unfolding—a spirituality that matures as you do, that shifts with time, and that keeps drawing you deeper.

A Heart-Centred Approach

Big Faith leads with the heart. It isn't just about what you believe in your mind—it's about what you feel, what you sense, and what moves you. This heart-centred approach welcomes your emotional and intuitive experiences. It says your tears, your wonder, your silence, and even your questions are all part of your faith. Spiritual writer Deepak Chopra describes spirituality as the experience of something beyond the physical and beyond the mind [3]. Big Faith listens to that experience. It knows that faith is often something you feel long before you can explain it. This makes space for mystery—for not needing to have all the answers. It encourages us to connect, not perform. To open up, not measure up. Faith, in this way, becomes a relationship, not a requirement. It becomes less about being right and more about being real. That's the power of Big Faith. It grows with you. It holds you. It frees you to meet God in ways you never expected—and in places you might have once overlooked

A Journey, Not a Destination

Big Faith understands that spirituality isn't something we arrive at—it's something we live. It grows with us. It changes shape as we change, deepening through our relationships, experiences, and the questions that arise along the way. Faith, in this sense, is not a fixed position, but a path that unfolds gradually, shaped by our willingness to walk it with openness and humility. Rather than being something we master, faith becomes something we return to—again and again. There are no final answers, only deeper invitations. When we let go of the pressure to have it all figured out, we make room for grace. We become more present to our own journey, more responsive to life as it is, and more attuned to what's sacred in the everyday.

The Importance of Experience and Practice

This journey of faith isn't sustained by belief alone—it's nurtured through lived practice. Big Faith is expressed in how we show up each day: how we listen, how we love, how we slow down enough to notice the divine woven into the ordinary. Whether through prayer, stillness, service, reflection, or silence, these practices are not about performance but presence. They are not rules to follow but rhythms that ground us— helping us reconnect when life feels scattered, and anchoring us in something deeper than the noise. These moments of intention help shape a faith that isn't abstract or distant, but real and relational. They remind us that faith is not about achieving certainty, but about choosing presence.

Ultimately, Big Faith invites us into a way of being that is alive, responsive, and evolving. It honours the truth that faith isn't a destination—it's a way of walking.

2. The Characteristics of Big Faith

A Deeper Look at What Shapes a Living, Expansive Faith

Big Faith carries qualities that breathe life into spirituality. It's not defined by rules or rigid doctrine, but by the posture of the heart— marked by courage, curiosity, compassion, and integrity. These characteristics create space for a deeper, more authentic way of engaging with the divine, with ourselves, and with others.

Courage and Vulnerability: Faith That Walks into the Unknown

Big Faith doesn't cling to certainty—it learns to stand in the unknown. It takes courage to ask questions without rushing to answers, and vulnerability to admit we don't have it all figured out. Yet this is where faith lives: in the tension, in the trust, in the willingness to keep walking forward without a map. As Parker Palmer reflects, *"The deeper our faith, the more doubts we must endure."* (Palmer, 2004) [4] Real faith isn't afraid of discomfort—it grows through it. Where traditional religion may insist on clarity and control, Big Faith welcomes the messiness of being human. In doing so, it allows for deeper resilience, openness, and transformation.

Open-Mindedness and Curiosity: Faith That Makes Room for Wonder

Big Faith is not afraid to wonder. It thrives on curiosity, inviting us to keep learning, unlearning, and growing. Rather than seeing questions as threats, it sees them as sacred invitations—to draw closer to the divine, to understand others more deeply, and to explore the mystery of life. Karen Armstrong reminds us that, *"Religion is not about believing things. It's about what you do and how you live."* (Armstrong, 2009) [5] This openness shifts the focus from rigid belief to a lived, evolving experience of the sacred. Big Faith opens the door to awe and mystery—reminding us that there's always more to discover, always more room for wonder.

Compassion and Empathy: Cultivating Connection and Shared Humanity

Big Faith cultivates a sense of connection and shared humanity, leading to greater empathy, kindness, and compassion. These are not surface-level virtues—they are transformative forces that reshape how we see others and ourselves. As Henri Nouwen writes, *"Compassion asks us to go where it hurts, to enter into the places of pain, to share in brokenness, fear, confusion, and anguish."* (Nouwen, 1983) [6]

This kind of compassion asks us to stay present in the discomfort, to listen deeply, and to honour the sacredness of another's story. When we are willing to be moved by another's pain or joy, we reflect the divine heartbeat of Big Faith. We become more attuned not only to the needs around us, but to the grace that flows through us. Rather than being rigid or self-righteous, Big Faith teaches us to respond with tenderness. It reminds us that true empathy is not just about agreeing—it's about understanding. When we cultivate compassion in this way, we help build a world marked not by judgment or exclusion, but by healing and wholeness.

Authenticity and Integrity: Living a Genuine and Wholehearted Life

Big Faith values honesty, depth, and alignment between who we are and how we live. It calls us to live with integrity—not as a performance, but as a reflection of what matters most to us. Authenticity is not about having it all together—it's about being true. When our outer life reflects our inner convictions, we create space for a life that feels rooted and whole. This kind of faith doesn't demand perfection. It invites presence. It asks us to examine whether we are living from our deepest values or simply following expectations. As Brené Brown puts it, *"Authenticity is the daily practice of letting go of who we think we're supposed to be and embracing who we are."* (Brown, 2010) [7] This practice is courageous. It requires self-awareness, honesty, and the willingness to live out what we believe even when it costs us. Integrity builds trust—in our relationships and within ourselves. It gives our faith credibility, not because we're flawless, but because we're faithful to what's real. Big Faith grows when we live with open hands and an honest heart.

3. Distinguishing Big Faith from Little Faith

A Qualitative vs. Quantitative Approach

The difference between Big Faith and Little Faith is not about who has more—it's about how we understand and live it. Little Faith is child-like faith, a "Yes Lord" faith, obedient faith, no questions asked faith, act upon it faith.

Big Faith on the other hand is measured in depth—in how it transforms you, how it roots you, and how it connects you to something greater. Big Faith doesn't ask, "Am I doing enough?" It asks, "Am I becoming whole?" It shifts the focus from performance to presence, from appearance to authenticity. It values how faith shapes your character, your relationships, and the way you show up in the world. As Søren Kierkegaard once wrote, *"The most painful state of being is remembering the future, particularly the one that never came to pass."* (Kierkegaard, 1843) [8] This reminder speaks to the danger of chasing imagined ideals instead of grounding ourselves in a faith that meets us here and now—in the present moment, in our lived reality. Big Faith recognises that everyone's spiritual path is different. It doesn't pressure you to measure up to someone else's experience. Instead, it honours your journey, your process, and your pace. Where religion seeks validation through external success, Big Faith grows quietly through inner transformation.

Fear-Based vs. Love-Based

Big Faith is rooted in life-affirming values like love, compassion, and connection. One of the clearest distinctions lies in what drives it: fear or love. Fear-based faith often emerges from anxiety, obligation, or the pressure to belong. It may lead individuals to cling to rigid beliefs out of a need for certainty or acceptance, rather than a genuine desire for spiritual growth.

When fear is the motivator, faith can become a source of stress and separation. It can reinforce division—between people, within communities, even within oneself. This kind of faith may leave individuals feeling judged, inadequate, or disconnected from those who believe differently. In contrast, love-based faith begins with connection—first to self, then to others, and then to something greater. Big Faith sees love as the truest foundation for spirituality. It invites people to grow, transform, and discover who they truly are. Where fear isolates, love unites. Where fear controls, love liberates. This kind of faith brings a sense of peace, compassion, and shared humanity. It also leads to movement. While fear keeps people stuck, love calls them forward. A faith rooted in love becomes a living, growing force. It nurtures resilience, kindness, and courage to face life honestly. It welcomes change and makes space for mystery and wonder. As spiritual writer Deepak Chopra expresses, *"The ultimate reality is not something that can be known through the senses or the mind, but it can be experienced through the heart."* (Chopra, 2000) [2]. This captures the essence of Big Faith—it's not about control or certainty, but about presence, openness, and love.

In the end, Big Faith calls us to let go of the fear that binds and embrace the love that frees. It's not about escaping struggle, but about choosing to walk through life with compassion, connection, and a heart that stays open—even in the unknown.

Static vs. Dynamic:

When faith becomes rigid and unchanging, it can lead to spiritual stagnation. People may begin to feel disconnected from their lived experience—from their emotions, questions, and inner knowing. This kind of rigidity often creates distance, not just internally but also in relationships, especially with those whose beliefs differ. Big Faith, by contrast, is dynamic. It moves with us. It recognises that spirituality is not a fixed set of answers but an unfolding journey. This posture makes space for growth, curiosity, and transformation. It welcomes the evolving nature of life and honours the personal nature of faith. When spirituality is allowed to be fluid and responsive, it becomes more inclusive and life-giving. Rather than shrinking faith down to creeds or formulas, Big Faith opens it up to experience, discovery, and connection. As Henri Nouwen once wrote, *"The spiritual life is not a life before, after, or beyond our everyday existence. No, the spiritual life can only be real when it is lived in the midst of the pains and joys of the here and now." (Nouwen, 1986)* [9]. Big Faith recognises this truth—it is grounded in real life, shaped by change, and responsive to the journey we are on. Rather than resisting growth, Big Faith embraces it. It allows us to remain anchored in what matters while staying open to new insight. In doing so, it nurtures a spiritual life that is resilient, compassionate, and alive—growing as we grow, shifting as we shift, always inviting us into deeper connection with the divine and with ourselves.

The Source of Big Faith

Where Does Big Faith Come From? The Power Of Inner Transformation

Big Faith is often born from a deep inner shift—a reorientation of how we see ourselves, God, and the world. It doesn't typically come from instruction alone but from experience. Sometimes, it begins in crisis. Sometimes, in stillness. But always, it starts within.

This kind of transformation can be sparked by a life-altering event: a diagnosis, a loss, a breakdown, or a breakthrough. Other times, it's less dramatic—a slow awakening, a quiet sense that the old ways no longer fit. Either way, something unsettles the surface and stirs the soul, calling us to go deeper.

As author and therapist James Hollis reflects, *"We are not here to fit in, be well balanced, or provide exemplars of normality. We are here to become more ourselves."* (Hollis, 2005) [1] That "becoming" often requires a confrontation with discomfort, a peeling back of inherited beliefs, and a willingness to look honestly at our lives. And yet, it's through this process that Big Faith is born—faith that isn't borrowed or performative, but rooted and real.

As former First Lady of the USA, Eleanor Roosevelt once said, *"You must do the thing you think you cannot do."* (Roosevelt, 1960) [2] This kind of deep inner shift is what often gives rise to Big Faith. It's not always born in comfort—but in those moments when we are called to face ourselves with courage. Inner transformation begins when we confront the limits of what we thought possible and allow something deeper, more enduring, to take root.

In other words, Big Faith isn't the absence of hardship—it's the presence of clarity. It's what happens when something shifts inside us, allowing us to see our lives with new eyes, and to live from a deeper place of trust. Inner transformation is rarely easy. It asks us to let go of what no longer serves us—old patterns, assumptions, even relationships. But what emerges in its place is something truer: a deeper self-awareness, a more open heart, and a clearer connection to what matters most. Big Faith doesn't arrive all at once. It unfolds. It's shaped by every moment that brings us closer to who we really are—and who God has always known us to be.

Life Experiences: Shaping and Strengthening Big Faith

The Influence of Role Models: Cultivating Big Faith Through Inspiration and Guidance

Inspiring role models, mentors, or spiritual leaders can have a profound impact on cultivating Big Faith. These individuals offer more than teaching—they offer presence. Their lives become a living invitation, calling us toward a deeper connection with ourselves, with others, and with God. By embodying the principles of Big Faith—compassion, empathy, courage, and kindness—they show what it looks like when faith becomes lived and visible. This influence is often most powerful in the early stages of spiritual formation. When someone is just beginning to question, to seek, or to wrestle with inherited beliefs, a trusted guide can bring calm to the chaos. Role models help us name our longing. They reflect back the possibility that faith can be authentic and real. They offer us language for what we didn't yet know how to say. They also help us stay the course. Even when faith feels fragile, their presence can give us strength. When we see someone living their faith with integrity—through suffering, through success, through silence—we are reminded that this path, though costly, is worth walking.

As spiritual leader the Dalai Lama once said, *"The ultimate source of happiness is not money and power, but warm-heartedness."* (Dalai Lama, 1999) [6]

That kind of warm-heartedness—tender but strong, soft but steady—is the very soil in which Big Faith grows. And when we witness it in someone else, it gives us the courage to cultivate it in ourselves.

The Role of Spirituality in Big Faith

Connecting to Something Greater

Spirituality plays a vital role in nurturing Big Faith. It invites us to connect with something beyond ourselves—God, the universe, or a deeper sense of transcendence. This connection offers meaning, purpose, and belonging. It reminds us that we are part of something larger, something sacred, something eternal.

As Henri Nouwen once wrote, *"Spiritual identity means we are not what we do or what people say about us. And we are not what we have. We are the beloved daughters and sons of God."* (Nouwen, 1992) [1] That identity forms the heart of Big Faith. It anchors us in something deeper than status or performance—it roots us in relationship. Spirituality opens us to mystery. It softens our certainty and makes room for awe. When we recognise the world as intricately woven—complex, beautiful, and alive—we begin to approach it with humility and reverence. This sense of wonder can awaken our faith, stirring something deep within that says, *"There is more."*

It also brings comfort. In moments of uncertainty, the awareness of something greater can offer peace that logic cannot. This grounding presence—whether we name it as God, Spirit, or simply "the More"—can carry us through grief, fear, and the unknown. Spirituality connects us not only to the divine, but to each other. When we find others who share our longing for meaning, we experience community. A shared practice or language of faith builds belonging—a place to be held, seen, and supported. This sacred connection strengthens our courage and expands our capacity for love.

In essence, spirituality stretches us beyond survival. It helps us transcend the limits of the self and discover a life anchored in presence, wonder, and trust. It is the heartbeat of Big Faith—reminding us that we are not alone, and that our story is part of something sacred and vast.

Exploring Spiritual Practices

Deepening One's Spiritual Connection and Cultivating Big Faith

Spiritual practices are not merely routines—they are sacred rhythms that help us return to ourselves and reconnect with the divine. Whether it's through meditation, prayer, journaling, or movement, these practices become gentle anchors, offering us comfort, clarity, and courage as we navigate life. As Deepak Chopra once wrote, *"Meditation is not a way to make your mind quiet; it's a way to enter into the quiet that's already there."* [9] In that quiet, faith begins to take root. Meditation helps us tune in to the still, steady presence beneath the noise. It invites us to rest—not just physically, but spiritually. When the world feels loud or uncertain, these quiet moments become a sanctuary. Prayer, too, offers more than words—it offers presence. It's less about performance and more about connection. In prayer, we speak honestly, listen openly, and lean into something greater than ourselves. Whether whispered or wordless, prayer reminds us we're not alone. Journaling brings reflection. It allows us to trace our own thoughts, feelings, and questions across the page. When we write from the heart, we often uncover the shape of our own faith—its wrestles, its hopes, its becoming. It is in these raw reflections that growth is often born. And then there's movement—whether it's yoga or simply walking in nature. Our bodies carry wisdom too. When we breathe deeply and move intentionally, we reconnect with the truth that we are whole beings: mind, body, and spirit. Spiritual practices do more than strengthen our faith—they sustain it. They create space for us to pause, listen, and be renewed. Over time, these practices help us become more present, more rooted, and more aware of the sacred within and around us.

These personal rhythms often extend into community. When we gather with others to practise, pray, or reflect, we begin to experience shared faith—not just individual belief. This sense of belonging reminds us that while the journey is personal, it's not solitary. Others are walking their own path too, and in shared spaces, we find encouragement, wisdom, and grace.

Ultimately, Big Faith is not a destination—it's a life lived in awareness. And spiritual practices are the steps we take to live it. They don't make us more 'spiritual'; they make us more attuned, more open, more alive to what's already true: that we are held, we are connected, and we are part of something bigger than ourselves.

The Power of Mindfulness: Cultivating Big Faith through Presence and Engagement

Mindfulness is more than a technique—it's a way of showing up to life. It teaches us to be fully here, in this moment, rather than distracted by what's behind us or anxious about what's ahead. In cultivating Big Faith, mindfulness becomes an essential practice. It helps us slow down, pay attention, and live from a deeper centre of awareness.

As Jon Kabat-Zinn reminds us, *"The best way to take care of the future is to take care of the present moment."* [8] This wisdom speaks directly to the heart of Big Faith. Rather than striving, striving, striving—we learn to stop, breathe, and notice. We begin to trust that meaning is not just out there waiting for us, but right here, in the now.

When we practise mindfulness, we become more aware of what's stirring within us—our thoughts, emotions, and bodily sensations. We learn to observe without judgment, to notice patterns, and to gently return to presence when we drift. Over time, this builds clarity. It helps us see not just what we're reacting to, but why. It deepens our self-understanding and our compassion for others.

Mindfulness also invites us into peace. Not the kind that comes from everything going right, but the kind that settles in when we stop running. It allows us to meet life as it is—with calm, with courage, with openness. And in that stillness, faith grows. It becomes less about control and more about surrender. Less about striving for answers and more about learning to be with the questions. Practising mindfulness can also shift how we relate to the world around us. As we become more present to the moment, we start to notice the sacred in the ordinary. A tree in the wind. A child's laughter. A quiet whisper of intuition. These small moments become doorways into wonder, gently reminding us that we are not separate, but part of something larger. This awareness anchors us. It keeps us from being swept away by fear or noise. And in that grounding, we find the strength to live intentionally—to act with love, to respond with grace, and to choose connection over reaction.

Ultimately, mindfulness makes space for Big Faith to flourish. It brings us back to ourselves, back to God, and back to the present moment—where life is lived, and where faith is found.

Nurturing Big Faith in Everyday Life

Integrating Spirituality into Daily Routine

Big Faith is not something reserved for rare moments or mountaintop experiences. It's shaped and strengthened in the everyday—in the ordinary rhythms of life. To nurture Big Faith, we must learn to weave spirituality into the fabric of our days, allowing it to become part of how we live, breathe, and respond. As Parker Palmer insightfully wrote, *"The spiritual life is not a separate compartment of our lives, but the very essence of our existence."* [5] This speaks to the heart of Big Faith. It's not an add-on or a special hour set aside each week. It's a way of being—present, aware, open. Simple practices, done consistently, can become anchors. Morning stillness. A midday pause to breathe. Gratitude at sunset. These small gestures can ground us, reminding us that we're not alone, and that life is sacred—even in its most mundane expressions.

For some, this might mean traditional spiritual disciplines like prayer, journaling, or scripture reflection. For others, it could be mindful walks in nature, lighting a candle in silence, or practising acts of kindness as devotion. What matters is not the form, but the intention behind it. The daily turning of the heart towards something greater. When spirituality is integrated into daily life, it creates a sense of rhythm—a steady undercurrent of presence and purpose. It can offer peace when the world feels chaotic, clarity when the path seems unclear, and resilience when challenges arise. Practices like gratitude and meditation have been shown to reduce stress and foster emotional well-being. But beyond the science, they carry a spiritual wisdom: they keep us connected—to God, to ourselves, and to the truth that we are held. Big Faith invites us to personalise this rhythm. There's no one-size-fits-all. Some may find spiritual resonance in yoga or mindful movement. Others may find it in daily affirmations or listening to music. The point is to explore, to be intentional, and to allow your faith to shape your habits—not just your beliefs.

In the end, nurturing Big Faith doesn't require grand gestures. It asks for presence. It asks for intention. And it asks us to show up—every day—with an open heart and a willingness to engage life spiritually, right where we are.

Cultivating a Sense of Wonder

The Key to Keeping Big Faith Alive and Vibrant

Big Faith thrives not just on knowledge or certainty—but on wonder. A living, vibrant faith is one that stays curious. It asks questions. It watches the sunrise and still feels moved. It allows room for mystery without needing to control the answers. Wonder keeps our faith tender, open, and alive. As religious scholar Karen Armstrong beautifully puts it, *"The sense of wonder is the beginning of all spirituality."* [10] Wonder invites us into the sacred, not as something to be mastered, but as something to behold. It calls us to pause, to breathe deeply, and to remember that there is more going on in this life than what we can explain or measure. When we engage the world through the lens of wonder, even the most ordinary moments become gateways to the divine. A child's laughter. The scent of rain. A quiet moment alone. These are not small things— they are sacred encounters. They reawaken us to the miracle of being here at all.

Wonder also keeps our hearts soft and our minds open. It frees us from the need to have it all figured out. It allows us to be learners again. And this is where Big Faith flourishes—not in rigid certainty, but in reverent exploration. When we stay curious, we stay connected. By contrast, religion—when driven by dogma—can sometimes suppress wonder. It can reward answers over questions and certainty over openness. But Big Faith invites the opposite. It welcomes the unknown. It celebrates mystery. It recognises that we don't grow by controlling life, but by surrendering to its beauty and unpredictability.

Cultivating wonder means letting life surprise you again. It means choosing to see the sacred in the everyday. It means asking, even when there are no neat answers. And it means embracing awe as a spiritual practice—one that keeps your faith from growing stale or brittle. Ultimately, wonder is what breathes life into Big Faith. It keeps us from closing in and invites us to open out. It keeps us wide-eyed, tender-hearted, and spiritually awake. And when wonder leads the way, faith becomes not just something we hold—but something that holds us.

Embracing Challenges as Opportunities

The Key to Nurturing Big Faith and Building Resilience

Big Faith is not just about belief—it's about how we live, especially when life gets hard. One of the most powerful ways to nurture this kind of faith is by learning to see challenges not as setbacks, but as sacred invitations to grow. When we face hardship with an open heart, we often discover strength, wisdom, and depth we never knew we had.

Psychologist and Holocaust survivor Viktor Frankl captured this truth powerfully: *"When we are no longer able to change a situation, we are challenged to change ourselves."* [3] Life won't always give us easy exits. But faith helps us choose how we show up in those moments. And that choice—to grow, to learn, to keep going—is what builds true resilience. Resilience isn't just bouncing back. It's being reshaped from the inside out. When we face difficulty with a posture of growth, we begin to develop deeper roots. We build a faith that's not afraid of pressure, but made stronger by it. In this way, our hardest seasons often become our most formative ones. This shift in perspective—seeing challenges as opportunities—also shapes how we understand purpose. Adversity presses us to reflect on what matters most. It clarifies our values and stirs our convictions. It asks us to decide who we want to be, not just when life is easy, but especially when it's not. Unlike rigid religion, which may treat suffering as something to fix, control, or avoid, Big Faith embraces the deeper invitation within it. It sees hardship as a teacher. It allows space for questions, for wrestling, and for transformation. It doesn't rush the process—it honours it.

Big Faith reminds us that difficulty doesn't have to break us. It can build us. It invites us to keep going not because we have all the answers, but because we've found something worth holding onto. Something within us—and beyond us—that keeps whispering, *"This isn't the end."*

Ultimately, embracing challenges as opportunities is a core practice of Big Faith. It teaches us to live with resilience, rootedness, and purpose. It reminds us that even in the darkest valleys, growth is possible—and that transformation often begins right where things feel the most uncertain.

CHAPTER 3

THE SHACKLES OF
TRADITIONAL RELIGION

The Constraints of Religion: Fear, Guilt, and the Stifling of Personal Growth

For many, religion has been more about control than connection. Instead of offering space for growth and transformation, it has too often relied on fear and guilt to shape behaviour. In this context, spirituality becomes less about love and more about punishment avoidance. Less about freedom—and more about fear. As psychologist Erich Fromm observed, *"The authoritarian conscience is not concerned with the act itself, but with its conformity to a rule."* (Fromm, 1950) [1] In religious settings, this kind of rigid obedience can smother authenticity. The focus shifts from inner transformation to external compliance. Rules are followed out of duty or fear, not devotion. The result? A stunted spiritual life that feels hollow rather than whole. When fear and guilt are the driving forces, shame is never far behind. Instead of cultivating a life-giving relationship with the divine, people often feel like they're constantly falling short—never quite worthy, never quite enough. This internal narrative can be crippling, leading to spiritual insecurity and a deep sense of unworthiness. You're not growing, you're just surviving. The danger lies in how this shapes a person's view of themselves—and of God. If your faith experience is defined by a list of infractions and the fear of punishment, there's little room for curiosity, joy, or genuine connection. The soul withdraws. Creativity is silenced. Individuality is treated as rebellion.

Big Faith invites us into something different. It doesn't diminish reverence or responsibility—it reclaims them. Not as chains, but as choices. It sees personal growth and spiritual freedom not as threats to God, but as reflections of His image in us. Big Faith makes space for questions, for wrestles, and for evolving truths. It invites us to bring our full selves—not just the parts that meet someone else's criteria.

Instead of shame, Big Faith offers dignity. Instead of fear, it offers love. And instead of rigid conformity, it welcomes a relationship that grows, deepens, and transforms us from the inside out.

Ultimately, the limitations of traditional religion reveal a deeper longing—for something more human, more hopeful, and more whole. By recognising the ways in which religion has confined and controlled, we begin to recover our freedom to believe differently, love more deeply, and reconnect with the sacred in ways that feel honest and alive.

Rigid Doctrine

The Constraints of Rigid Doctrine: Limiting Exploration and Critical Thinking in Religion

Rigid doctrine has long been a cornerstone of institutional religion—but it often comes at a cost. When belief becomes fixed, and questioning is discouraged, spiritual life starts to shrink. Instead of inviting people into deeper wonder or discovery, religion can become a gatekeeper of what is "right," narrowing the path instead of widening it.

As religious scholar Karen Armstrong notes, *"The tendency to dogmatism is a fundamentalist trait."* (Armstrong, 2009) [2] In this kind of environment, belief stops being a living, evolving conversation—and becomes a set of immovable rules. People begin to measure their worth by how well they conform, rather than how deeply they connect. There's little room for curiosity, no space for dissent, and certainly no grace for questions that don't have neat answers. This dogmatic mindset often suppresses critical thinking. When new perspectives are seen as threats, rather than invitations to grow, dialogue disappears. Those who dare to question are seen as dangerous, disloyal, or lost. But in truth, the desire to explore is not a sign of weak faith—it's the sign of a living one. Without room to reflect, challenge, or change, faith becomes static. And when it becomes static, it starts to lose its power to inspire. Big Faith takes a different view. It doesn't demand blind allegiance to inherited systems. It invites you to wrestle, to reason, and to grow. It recognises that spirituality is not a one-size-fits-all path. Instead, it's dynamic—shaped by seasons, questions, and the unfolding of personal experience. Big Faith values mystery over mastery. It knows that God is not threatened by our questions—and that real understanding often begins with uncertainty.

By freeing ourselves from the constraints of rigid doctrine, we make space for a more generous, inclusive spirituality—one where critical thinking and compassion can walk hand in hand. One where doubt isn't the enemy of faith, but part of its deepening.

Ultimately, Big Faith isn't about memorising dogma. It's about staying awake. It's about choosing discovery over defensiveness. And it's about allowing your faith to breathe, evolve, and reflect the depth and complexity of your own human experience.

Conformity Over Creativity

The Stifling of Personal Growth and Autonomy

When religion prizes conformity over authenticity, something vital is lost. The invitation to grow, create, and explore becomes muted beneath the pressure to behave, believe, and belong in specific, acceptable ways. In these environments, individuality is often sacrificed for uniformity—and the result is a kind of spiritual stagnation. As psychologist Abraham Maslow observed, *"The most creative people are those who are most able to tolerate ambiguity."* (Maslow, 1962) [3] But institutional religion often resists ambiguity. It seeks certainty. It prefers answers over questions, alignment over originality. In doing so, it discourages the very kind of inner exploration that is essential for deep and lasting transformation. When individuals are taught to suppress their own voice in order to echo another's, spiritual autonomy fades. The path becomes less about connection and more about compliance. The beauty of personal discovery is replaced by a checklist of approved behaviours. And in that space, creativity—the lifeblood of spiritual vitality—gets pushed aside. This emphasis on conformity also impacts community. When everyone is expected to look, act, and believe the same way, diversity becomes a threat rather than a strength. Those who don't fit the mould—whether because of background, belief, orientation, or simply personality—can feel alienated or silenced. A space that was meant to nurture the soul ends up policing it instead. Big Faith offers an alternative. It celebrates creativity as a sacred expression. It encourages the artist, the questioner, the quiet thinker, and the passionate reformer. Rather than punishing difference, it welcomes it. Big Faith understands that spiritual maturity often means holding space for what we don't yet understand—and finding God not just in clarity, but also in complexity. Rather than demanding blind allegiance, Big Faith invites honest exploration. It welcomes spiritual practices that are personal and evolving, not performative or static. It encourages us to find our voice, to create freely, and to live our faith in ways that are deeply aligned with who we are becoming. Ultimately, the stifling of creativity and autonomy under religious conformity reveals the need for a broader, more compassionate path— one that allows space for uniqueness, honours imagination, and recognises that true spiritual growth is both deeply personal and endlessly unfolding.

How Religion Can Stifle Growth

The Dangers of Spiritual Stagnation

When spirituality becomes static, it loses its power to transform. Religion, when overly focused on rigid doctrine and repetition, can quietly lead to stagnation. What begins as devotion can devolve into duty—leaving people spiritually dry, emotionally disengaged, and distant from their inner life. This kind of spiritual paralysis is not always loud, but it is deeply erosive. Psychologist Carl Jung observed, *"**The most important thing in life is to learn how to give out love, and let it come in." (Jung, 1964)** [4]* Love—freely given and received—is the beating heart of spiritual vitality. But when religion becomes primarily about performance or compliance, the flow of love can be blocked. In such systems, the soul is often taught to behave rather than to blossom. Rigid structures may offer stability, but they can also become cages. People begin to repeat rituals that no longer move them. They speak words that no longer speak to them. Instead of growing, they plateau.

Instead of evolving, they shrink. Instead of expanding, they withdraw. Spiritual stagnation doesn't mean someone has lost faith—it often means their faith has lost movement. When religion discourages questioning, doubt, or imagination, people disconnect not only from the divine but from themselves. They go through the motions but feel empty inside. What once was sacred becomes stale.

Big Faith offers a different path. It invites movement, not just maintenance. It values transformation over tradition, not by discarding the past, but by letting spirituality breathe in the present. Big Faith encourages reflection, creativity, and honest connection with both God and self. It trusts that spiritual growth comes through curiosity, not just compliance.

Where religion may say "stay in line," Big Faith says "step into the unknown." Where religion demands conformity, Big Faith nurtures authenticity. It's not about abandoning sacred truths, but about allowing them to come alive in new ways—through love, through wonder, and through lived experience.

Ultimately, the danger of spiritual stagnation is not just that we stop growing, but that we stop seeking. By reclaiming a faith that grows with us—not against us—we open ourselves to deeper connection, renewed purpose, and the kind of love that truly transforms.

Missed Opportunities

The Consequences of Religion's Narrow Focus
When spirituality becomes boxed into rigid rules and prescribed beliefs, it often misses the quiet invitations to grow, explore, and live with depth. Religion, with its emphasis on conformity and tradition, can unintentionally stifle the human spirit. Instead of drawing people into

the fullness of life, it can lead them into a version of faith that feels safe, but not alive. As Parker Palmer writes, *"The most important thing in life is to learn how to live in the present moment."* (Palmer, 2004) [5] In the present moment, we encounter clarity. We meet ourselves honestly. We access creativity, insight, and courage. But when we're taught to follow rather than to reflect, that sacred moment often slips past us. Religion's focus on what was, or what must be, can make it difficult to fully live what is. When individuals are expected to prioritise obedience over authenticity, they may begin to feel disconnected from their true desires and dreams. They do what is expected—yet feel unfulfilled. Their lives move forward, but their spirits remain untouched. Over time, the disconnect between outward compliance and inward longing breeds frustration, even despair. Missed opportunities aren't always dramatic. Sometimes they look like a song never sung, a calling never pursued, or a truth never spoken aloud. These quiet sacrifices—made to meet religious expectations—can accumulate into a life that feels half-lived.

Big Faith responds differently. It doesn't fear the unknown. It welcomes the present moment and sees it as sacred ground. Rather than discouraging individuality, Big Faith celebrates it. It invites people to bring their full selves—questions, creativity, convictions—into their spiritual life. It doesn't demand that people fit a mould; it trusts that the Spirit speaks uniquely to every heart.

By letting go of rigid conformity and embracing a more present, open, and courageous way of being, we reclaim the opportunities religion often causes us to miss. We become available to wonder. We listen more deeply. We live more fully.

Ultimately, a narrow version of religion can lead to a narrow version of life. But Big Faith keeps the soul awake. It invites us to grow not by rule, but by resonance—to live not merely in tradition, but in truth.

Unrealised Potential

The Constraints of Religion

Religion, when centred on conformity and control, can become a barrier to personal growth. Rather than nurturing the gifts and passions within each person, it can suppress them—limiting the imagination, silencing the dreamer, and slowing down the soul's journey. Religion often demands allegiance to tradition over the exploration of one's own calling. As Viktor Frankl wrote, *"The greatest discovery of any generation is that a human being can alter his life by altering his attitudes."* (Frankl, 1946) [6] When our mindset is fixed—rooted in fear, shame, or unquestioned dogma—we lose the freedom to imagine a different life. Possibility begins in the mind, and without that, potential lies dormant. The tragedy of unrealised potential isn't just personal— it's spiritual. When someone is told their deepest desires are distractions or that their gifts don't fit within a religious framework, it creates an inner dissonance. They may attend, obey, and serve—yet inwardly feel unfulfilled, as if they're living someone else's version of faith.

Big Faith offers another way. It welcomes a growth mindset. It tells the seeker: *Your questions matter. Your gifts are needed. Your story belongs.* Rather than demanding conformity, it invites discovery. Big Faith sees spirituality not as a fixed destination, but as an unfolding path—a space where individuals can grow into their calling and respond to the divine in ways that are real and personal. This approach empowers people to find purpose not through pressure, but through presence. It doesn't silence dreams—it sanctifies them. It understands that meaning isn't handed down through doctrine alone but discovered through the journey of becoming fully alive. When spirituality is no longer about fitting in, but about becoming whole, people begin to rise. They take risks. They create. They heal. They lead. That's what happens when faith liberates rather than limits.

Ultimately, the constraints of Religion reveal a deeper need—a need to recover a faith that calls forth potential, honours uniqueness, and empowers people to live fully and freely. Big Faith does just that.

Breaking Free from the Chains of Dogma

The Power of Questioning Authority

To nurture a faith that is alive, personal, and expansive, one must first be willing to question. Breaking free from the chains of religious dogma begins with curiosity—a quiet rebellion that refuses to accept inherited truths without first testing them. It requires courage to challenge what has long been considered sacred, but in doing so, individuals step into a more authentic and liberating spiritual journey.

As philosopher Alan Watts once wrote, *"No valid plans for the future can be made by those who have no capacity for living now."* (Watts, 1951) [7]. This insight reminds us that religious systems fixated on rigid futures can rob us of the present moment—and with it, the chance to explore, wrestle, and wonder. When faith is reduced to a checklist of beliefs, we risk missing the real encounter with the divine that only happens when we are present, awake, and searching. Religion often discourages inquiry. It teaches obedience over exploration and prioritises external authority over inner conviction. In this environment, people learn to silence their doubts and submit their questions, fearing that to ask is to rebel. Yet, true growth—both personal and spiritual—demands the opposite.

Questioning authority is not an act of rebellion for its own sake, but an act of reverence for truth. When individuals challenge assumptions and examine their beliefs honestly, they begin to move from inherited religion to lived faith. They no longer follow out of fear, but pursue truth out of love. This shift opens the door to a spirituality grounded not in dogma, but in discovery.

Big Faith encourages this kind of sacred questioning. It understands that faith deepens not in the absence of doubt, but through the process of wrestling with it. It invites the seeker to take ownership of their spiritual life—to ask hard questions, to sit with mystery, to explore new paths. This approach honours the uniqueness of every soul and gives people the freedom to evolve. Moreover, the act of questioning builds integrity. When individuals learn to trust their inner wisdom, they cultivate self-respect and clarity. This inner authority empowers them to form deeper, more honest relationships with others—no longer needing to perform or pretend in order to belong.

Ultimately, breaking free from the chains of dogma is not about rejecting all that came before. It is about discerning what truly gives life. It's about replacing fear with freedom, rules with relationship, and silence with sacred conversation. When people begin to ask real questions, they begin to live a real faith—one that is bold, evolving, and unmistakably their own.

Embracing Uncertainty

The Power of Ambiguity and Paradox in the Spiritual Journey

To walk a genuine spiritual path is to make peace with mystery. Embracing uncertainty, ambiguity, and paradox is not a detour from faith—it is faith. When we stop insisting on clear-cut answers and allow ourselves to live inside the questions, something shifts. We move from grasping for certainty to standing in awe of life's depth, complexity, and wonder.

As theologian Paul Tillich reflects, *"The courage to be is the courage to accept the uncertainty of the future."* (Tillich, 1957) [8] This insight speaks directly to the heart of Big Faith. It takes courage to release our grip on what is fixed and familiar. Yet in doing so, we discover a richer, more expansive way of being—one that invites us to trust, not because we understand, but because we are willing to journey forward without needing to.

Traditional religion often struggles with ambiguity. It seeks to resolve mystery with answers and reinforce belief with certainty. But in doing so, it can flatten the spiritual landscape into rules and absolutes. While clarity can bring comfort, it can also create a kind of spiritual rigidity that leaves no room for the unknown, the evolving, or the deeply personal.

Big Faith invites us into a different posture—one of openness, not closure. It honours the paradoxes of life: strength found in surrender, presence found in stillness, wisdom born of not knowing. By letting go of the need to be right or certain, we step into something far greater than knowledge—we step into trust.

This embrace of ambiguity also cultivates humility. It reminds us that we do not have all the answers, and perhaps we were never meant to. When we admit our limits, we make room for wonder. And wonder, unlike certainty, keeps the heart open and the spirit awake. It draws us deeper, not into dogma, but into awe.

To live with Big Faith is not to abandon reason or discernment. It is to hold our beliefs with a gentle grip, allowing space for growth, for mystery, and for change. It is to remain teachable, even when we are seasoned. It is to say, "I don't know, but I am willing to walk forward anyway."

Ultimately, embracing uncertainty is not about being adrift—it's about being anchored in trust rather than answers. It's the kind of faith that flourishes not because everything is clear, but because we are willing to remain present in the midst of what is not. This is the quiet strength of Big Faith: it thrives in the unknown, nourished by awe and rooted in courage.

Finding Personal Truth

A Journey of Self-Discovery and Spiritual Growth

Finding personal truth is not about arriving at a final answer—it's about learning how to listen. It is a journey marked by honesty, self-reflection, and the quiet courage to trust your own inner voice. Unlike inherited doctrines or external expectations, personal truth emerges through lived experience, through the deep work of paying attention to what resonates in your soul. As spiritual teacher Deepak Chopra reminds us, **"The ultimate truth is not something that can be found; it is something that can be experienced."** (Chopra, 2000) [9] This experience cannot be borrowed or handed down—it must be encountered firsthand, felt deeply, and lived out in real time. True spiritual growth begins when you stop looking for the 'right answer' out there and begin discovering the truth that already lives within you. The path to personal truth is intimate and evolving. It asks you to sit with your own values, question what you've been taught, and sift through the layers of assumption and fear until you find what is real for you. It requires patience—there are no shortcuts. But the fruit of this journey is profound: a life that aligns with your inner knowing, not just outer approval. Religion, when rigid and prescriptive, often discourages this kind of exploration. It can reduce spirituality to a list of correct beliefs and behaviours, offering certainty in exchange for obedience. But in doing so, it risks disconnecting people from their own spiritual instincts and silencing the deeper questions that lead to growth.

Big Faith offers another way. It trusts that God is not threatened by our questions, that the Spirit often whispers in doubt as much as in certainty. It gives us room to wrestle, to explore, and to arrive at faith not as something we inherit blindly, but as something we encounter honestly. In this way, Big Faith honours the journey over the formula. When we begin to live from our personal truth, we also begin to live with more self-trust. We become more anchored in who we are, more confident in the choices we make, and more gracious with others on their own journeys. We stop needing to perform spirituality for others and instead embody it from a place of sincerity and depth. Finding personal truth doesn't mean walking away from tradition—it means walking deeper into your own integrity. It means holding space for nuance, allowing your understanding to evolve, and letting your faith be shaped by both experience and reflection.

Ultimately, discovering personal truth is an act of spiritual liberation. It's the unfolding of a practice that is yours—honest, rooted, and alive. And when you walk in that truth, you do more than find yourself. You begin to find God in a new way, too.

CHAPTER 4

THE DANGERS OF BLIND OBEDIENCE

---

1. The Risks of Unquestioning Faith and Blind Loyalty

Unquestioning faith can feel comforting. It often provides a sense of belonging, stability, and spiritual reassurance. But when faith goes unchecked—when beliefs are never examined and loyalty becomes blind—it can become dangerous. Blind obedience can cause people to follow harmful or oppressive teachings without thinking them through. Over time, this can weaken a person's sense of right and wrong, and limit their ability to think for themselves (Fromm, 1950) [1]. Psychologist Erich Fromm observed, *"The authoritarian personality is characterized by a tendency to submit to authority and to conform to the expectations of others."* (Fromm, 1950) [1] His words reveal how easily people can hand over their autonomy to those in power. When that happens, individuals can become vulnerable—emotionally, spiritually, and even physically. They may find themselves manipulated or controlled, unable to recognise when something is wrong because they've been taught not to question it. This kind of obedience is especially risky in religious environments. People are often told to follow doctrines without question, trust leaders without hesitation, and accept teachings without reflection. But when faith becomes passive like this, people lose their connection to their own inner compass. As Fromm also wrote, *"The surrender of autonomy is often accompanied by a sense of relief, as the individual is no longer responsible for making decisions or taking responsibility for their actions."* (Fromm, 1950) [1] While that kind of relief might feel comforting at first, it rarely lasts. Sooner or later, the cost of blind loyalty becomes clear—whether through personal disillusionment or real harm.

Blind obedience also holds people back from growing spiritually. When we stop thinking critically, we stop learning. Faith becomes static. People begin to repeat beliefs they've inherited, rather than discovering what rings true for them. But when we allow space for reflection—when we question, explore, and even wrestle with what we believe—we begin to develop a deeper, more personal connection with our spirituality. This kind of faith is not only more resilient, but also more real.

That's why **Big Faith** invites us to question, to think, and to grow. It values maturity over mindless loyalty, and experience over inherited rules. It asks us to build our beliefs on personal conviction rather than passive acceptance. **Religion**, by contrast, often discourages questions. It prefers submission over exploration, and in doing so, limits both the spirit and the soul.

Ultimately, the dangers of blind obedience serve as a caution. Faith should not mean surrendering your ability to think, feel, and discern. As Fromm wisely noted, *"The development of autonomy and critical thinking is essential for the development of a healthy and mature personality."* (Fromm, 1950) [1] In other words, true faith grows best in the soil of freedom, reflection, and responsibility.

Loss of Autonomy: The Consequences of Blind Obedience

Blind obedience, though often praised as loyalty or submission, can slowly strip away a person's autonomy and sense of self. When individuals hand over their decision-making power to authority figures or religious doctrine, they begin to lose connection with their inner voice. Over time, this can lead to a diminished sense of self, a weakening of personal responsibility, and a deep reliance on external direction (Maslow, 1962) [2]. As psychologist Abraham Maslow warned, "To be self-actualised is to be fully human, to function according to one's full potential." (Maslow, 1962) [2] This highlights the essential role of personal awareness and autonomy in growth. True spiritual life requires presence, agency, and inner freedom—qualities that erode when one's choices are constantly filtered through someone else's expectations or approval. When blind obedience becomes the default posture, people can feel powerless in their own lives. Decisions are no longer personal but prescribed. Actions are motivated not by discernment but by duty or fear. Over time, this disconnection can hollow out the soul. Individuals may begin to feel like passive participants in their own stories, unsure of their values, uncertain of their desires, and distant from their purpose.

The emotional cost is steep. A lack of autonomy often leads to increased stress, anxiety, and depression. The more someone becomes reliant on external guidance, the less they trust their own instincts. Self-esteem declines. Confidence wavers. Personal agency shrinks. And instead of growing in wisdom and maturity, the person becomes increasingly mechanical—carrying out rituals, reciting beliefs, and performing roles without inner alignment. In the framework of *Big Faith*, this is precisely what must be challenged. Big Faith calls individuals to spiritual maturity—not by dictating what to believe, but by empowering them to explore, reflect, and choose for themselves. It promotes a spirituality that is thoughtful, grounded, and self-aware. By encouraging discernment and autonomy, Big Faith helps individuals cultivate a deeper sense of responsibility for their own growth, relationships, and life direction.

Religion, in contrast, often demands conformity. It frames obedience as a virtue while dismissing doubt or questioning as dangerous. This leads not only to external control, but to internal disconnection—a kind of spiritual numbness that dulls passion, creativity, and authenticity. In the end, the loss of autonomy that results from blind obedience should serve as a warning. True spiritual growth cannot happen in the absence of personal agency. As Maslow warned, *"**The greatest danger to humanity is the tendency to surrender to the automatic, the mechanical, and the robotic.**"* (Maslow, 1962) [2]. The spiritual life is not meant to be robotic—it is meant to be alive, thoughtful, engaged, and free.

Vulnerability to Manipulation: The Risks of Surrendering Critical Thinking

When individuals set aside their critical thinking, they open themselves to a dangerous vulnerability—one that can be exploited emotionally, psychologically, and even financially. Without discernment, it becomes far easier to be pulled into harmful behaviours or belief systems that serve someone else's agenda rather than one's own well-being (Langone, 2000) [3]. In such a state, decisions are made not with clarity or conviction, but through manipulation, fear, or pressure. As cult expert Michael Langone observes, *"The most effective way to manipulate people is to appeal to their emotions rather than their reason."* (Langone, 2000) [3]. This insight captures the essence of how manipulation operates: it bypasses reason and targets the heart, often masquerading as spiritual urgency or moral duty. Once emotions are triggered and rational thought is suspended, people can be led to act against their own values, beliefs, and best interests.

The results can be deeply damaging. Individuals may find themselves caught up in groupthink, carrying out actions they later regret, or making sacrifices—emotional, financial, even physical—that leave them harmed or depleted. What begins as trust or loyalty can quickly become coercion. And in many cases, the manipulation is cloaked in religious language, making it harder to recognise and even harder to resist. But the consequences don't stop with the individual. When groups of people are swayed by emotional manipulation, the ripple effects can spread outward—causing social division, economic harm, or even violence. History bears witness to the ways that blind allegiance, cloaked in moral or spiritual justification, can lead entire communities into harm.

Big Faith, by contrast, insists on the value of discernment. It encourages believers to test what they hear, weigh what they're told, and hold every teaching up to the light of love, wisdom, and reason. It nurtures a spirituality that is both heartfelt and thoughtful, grounded in empathy but protected by awareness. It equips individuals not only to believe, but to choose—to stay present, to ask questions, and to say no when something doesn't resonate with truth.

Religion, on the other hand, often thrives on emotionalism and unchecked authority. It encourages loyalty over learning, compliance over curiosity. And in doing so, it makes people easier to control, easier to exploit, and less likely to speak up when something feels wrong. The risk of manipulation is a call to vigilance.

Faith should not mean the end of thought. Spirituality should not require the suspension of one's mind. As Langone reminds us, *"Critical thinking is the best defense against manipulation and exploitation."* (Langone, 2000) [3]. By cultivating discernment and staying rooted in both love and reason, we protect not only our minds, but our integrity, our voice, and our freedom.

2. The Importance of Critical Thinking in Faith

Informed Decision-Making

Critical thinking plays a vital role in a healthy spiritual life. It allows individuals to examine evidence, weigh arguments, and make thoughtful, informed decisions about their faith, values, and spiritual practices. Rather than blindly accepting teachings, the practice of discernment helps believers navigate the complexities of spiritual life with clarity, depth, and integrity (Armstrong, 2009) [4]. This approach includes reflecting on spiritual teachings, questioning the credibility of spiritual leaders, and engaging with multiple perspectives. In doing so, individuals learn not only what they believe, but *why* they believe it. Critical thinking is not the enemy of faith—it is its companion. It keeps the spiritual path honest, reflective, and alive.

Without this faculty, people are more vulnerable to manipulation or exploitation. They may be easily swayed by persuasive leaders, charismatic doctrines, or emotional appeals. They may even confuse truth with tradition, and passion with authenticity. But critical thinking provides the tools to distinguish the authentic from the inauthentic, the essential from the peripheral.

As religious scholar Karen Armstrong reminds us, *"The critical faculty is essential to the spiritual life, for it enables us to distinguish between the essential and the peripheral."* (Armstrong, 2009) [4]. Her words challenge the idea that real faith must be passive or unthinking. In fact, true spiritual maturity demands that we reflect, wrestle, and ask hard questions. This kind of inquiry deepens spiritual understanding and fosters personal growth. It encourages individuals to bring their full selves—mind and heart—into their spiritual journey. In doing so, faith becomes a lived experience, not a static set of inherited rules. It becomes about *relationship* rather than ritual, *transformation* rather than tradition. Critical thinking also fosters empathy and tolerance. By considering diverse spiritual perspectives with openness and care, individuals develop a more expansive understanding of truth.

They see that there is wisdom to be gleaned from many traditions, and that spirituality is not a one-size-fits-all path.

In contrast, *Religion* often discourages this kind of thinking. It equates questioning with rebellion and elevates obedience over curiosity. It prefers conformity to contemplation. But in doing so, it stunts spiritual growth, reduces faith to dogma, and diminishes the believer's sense of agency.

Big Faith, on the other hand, values informed belief. It welcomes questions. It encourages each individual to be a seeker, to remain awake and engaged, and to integrate their values with their intellect. As

Armstrong writes, *"Critical thinking is not an enemy of faith, but a friend, for it enables us to discern the truth and to distinguish between the authentic and the counterfeit."* (Armstrong, 2009) [4]. critical thinking is not a threat to spiritual life—it is a lifeline. It enables individuals to grow into a faith that is strong yet open, rooted yet evolving. It helps them take ownership of their beliefs, and to walk their path with discernment, freedom, and responsibility. In a world of competing claims and shifting ideologies, it may be one of the most sacred tools we have.

Discernment and Reflection

Discernment and reflection are essential components of a spiritually mature life. They allow individuals to thoughtfully evaluate the teachings they receive, the leaders they follow, and the practices they adopt. This isn't about constant scepticism—it's about spiritual attentiveness. It's the willingness to pause, reflect, and weigh what is being taught against one's lived experience, values, and spiritual convictions (Palmer, 2004) [5]. Parker Palmer puts it clearly: *"Discernment is the process of distinguishing between the authentic and the counterfeit, the true and the false."* (Palmer, 2004) [5] In a world saturated with voices and platforms, this process is more crucial than ever. Without it, one risks mistaking charisma for character, tradition for truth, or noise for wisdom. Discernment is not a quick decision or a gut reaction. It is slow work. It requires silence, patience, and a commitment to truth over convenience. Through regular reflection, individuals begin to recognise what aligns with their spiritual integrity—and what does not. This becomes the foundation for a faith that is not only informed but anchored.

Spiritual Maturity: The Fruit of Critical Thinking and Nuanced Understanding

Spiritual maturity is a hallmark of an authentic and deeply rooted faith. It is not something achieved in a moment, but the result of a lifelong process of growth, reflection, and courageous exploration. Rather than blind adherence to doctrine, it requires the ability to hold complexity, ask honest questions, and seek truth beyond the surface.

Critical thinking plays a vital role in this journey. It sharpens discernment, strengthens conviction, and equips individuals to navigate life's moral and spiritual complexities with wisdom and grace. Those who think deeply and engage honestly with their faith are not weakened by questions—they are strengthened by them. Over time, this leads to a more informed and integrated understanding of both their beliefs and themselves (Chopra, 2000) [6]. As Deepak Chopra puts it, *"Spiritual maturity is the ability to see the world from multiple perspectives and to find the truth in all of them."* (Chopra, 2000) [6] This speaks to the openness and humility that define a mature faith—one that is not threatened by difference, but enriched by it. Spiritual maturity allows for nuance, welcomes ambiguity, and honours the mystery that lies at the heart of true spirituality. Those who embody this maturity are often marked by compassion, clarity, and calm. They don't rush to judgement or cling to easy answers. Instead, they remain present to the deeper currents beneath life's events, aware that truth is rarely simple and growth often comes through tension. This capacity to hold paradox and to see beauty in complexity is a sign of wisdom and spiritual depth.

At its core, spiritual maturity is also shaped by humility. Those who possess it are deeply aware of the limitations of their own understanding, and as a result, they carry a posture of curiosity and wonder. They remain open to growth, willing to learn from others, and responsive to new insights. This openness creates space for ongoing transformation.

In contrast, *Religion* often discourages this kind of depth. It values certainty over curiosity, and conformity over growth. By promoting rigid boundaries and unquestioned beliefs, it can trap people in a shallow understanding of faith—one that resists change and fears doubt. But Big Faith invites us to something deeper. It honours the personal journey, embraces complexity, and fosters the courage to keep growing.

In essence, spiritual maturity is not a destination but a way of travelling. It is a lifelong journey of becoming—grounded in reflection, strengthened by truth, and guided by love. As Chopra reminds us, *"Spiritual maturity is not a destination, but a journey. It is a journey of discovery, of growth, and of transformation."* (Chopra, 2000) [6]

Finding Balance Between Faith and Reason

Integrating Head and Heart

True spiritual growth involves more than belief or logic—it's a delicate weaving together of thought and feeling, reason and faith. For centuries, people have debated whether faith and reason can coexist. Some have insisted they are at odds, while others argue that they complement one another. In reality, a rich spiritual life requires both. It calls for the clear discernment of the head and the deep sensitivity of the heart (Wilber, 1996) [7]. As philosopher Ken Wilber writes, *"The integration of the head and heart is essential for spiritual growth and transformation."* (Wilber, 1996) [7] His words remind us that neither side—intellect nor intuition—can carry the full weight of faith alone. It's in their meeting place that genuine transformation happens. The intellect brings clarity. It enables us to examine beliefs, question assumptions, and reflect critically on our practices. It helps us grow in wisdom, make sound decisions, and avoid being led astray by emotion or misinformation. But without the heart, the spiritual journey risks becoming cold, abstract, and disconnected—rich in doctrine, but poor in love. The heart, on the other hand, offers us access to emotion, empathy, and the intuitive knowing that often leads us into deeper connection—with God, with others, and with ourselves. It stirs compassion and fosters the kind of presence that reason alone cannot offer. Yet, unchecked, the heart can also lead us into sentimentality, bypassing the need for grounded discernment. That is why integration is so vital. When the head and heart work together, our faith becomes both thoughtful and tender. We can think deeply without becoming rigid, and feel deeply without losing clarity. This union creates space for a more complete experience of the spiritual life—one that honours both intellect and intuition, both conviction and compassion.

This balance also equips us to hold the tension and paradox of the spiritual path. Not every mystery needs solving, and not every feeling needs to become a belief. When both heart and head are honoured, we can live with open questions, welcome complexity, and extend grace—to ourselves and to others.

Religion, however, often leans too far in one direction. Some expressions become overly intellectual, reducing faith to doctrine and debate. Others swing the opposite way, relying solely on emotional fervour while neglecting thoughtful engagement. Either imbalance can stunt growth and limit depth.

Big Faith calls us to more. It invites us to bring our whole selves into the spiritual journey—our minds and our emotions, our logic and our longing. It honours both contemplation and compassion, analysis and awe. **This integration doesn't happen overnight; it is, as Wilber reminds us, "a dynamic process that requires ongoing effort and commitment."** (Wilber, 1996) [7]

When we learn to live with both clarity and warmth, both insight and intuition, we find ourselves rooted in something deeper than certainty—we become anchored in truth that is alive, whole, and transforming.

Embracing Paradox

The Key to Spiritual Maturity

To grow in faith is to grow comfortable with tension—the tension between knowing and not knowing, between certainty and mystery. Spiritual maturity does not come from resolving every contradiction, but from learning to hold opposing truths with grace and openness. Embracing paradox becomes not just an invitation but a requirement for those who long for a deeper, fuller life of faith. Theologian Paul Tillich once wrote, **"The paradox is the essence of the spiritual life, for it represents the tension between the finite and the infinite."** (Tillich, 1957) [8] His words capture a profound truth: that the spiritual journey is not neat or simple. It is layered, mysterious, and at times, filled with questions that don't have clear answers. Paradox shows up everywhere in faith: we are both broken and beloved. God is both just and merciful. We are called to surrender and to act. These tensions are not mistakes to fix but mysteries to inhabit. Spiritual depth comes not from explaining paradoxes away, but from allowing them to shape us—from learning to trust that some truths are bigger than our ability to fully understand them. In these moments, certainty can be a poor substitute for awe. While rigid doctrine often tries to solve every mystery, Big Faith invites us to live within them. It encourages us to hold space for ambiguity, not as weakness, but as wisdom. When we stop demanding black-and-white answers, we become more present, more open, and more able to see God's hand in places we once overlooked. This posture also fosters compassion. When we recognise that life is filled with complexity, we become slower to judge and quicker to listen. We stop needing to defend our position at every turn and start seeking understanding. Embracing paradox allows us to honour the differences in belief, experience, and perspective that shape the lives of others. It makes room for empathy and invites unity without uniformity. Religion often demands resolution—clear answers, fixed categories, firm lines. But Big Faith recognises that the deepest truths are often held in tension. It teaches us to trust the process, to let mystery be our teacher, and to accept that not everything sacred can be simplified. As Tillich reminds us, ***"The paradox is not a problem to be solved, but a mystery to be lived."*** (Tillich, 1957) [8] And in learning to live the mystery, we grow—not just in understanding, but in humility, compassion, and depth of soul.

Cultivating Humility

The Foundation of Spiritual Growth

At the heart of any meaningful spiritual journey lies humility. It is not weakness or self-deprecation, but an honest recognition of our human limitations and a deep reverence for the vastness of what we do not yet know. Cultivating humility allows us to stay open—to keep learning, unlearning, and growing as we walk the path of faith. Philosopher Søren Kierkegaard once said, *"The most important thing in life is to learn how to be humble, for humility is the foundation of all spiritual growth."* (Kierkegaard, 1843) [9] His words remind us that true spiritual depth doesn't begin with certainty, but with curiosity—with the kind of posture that kneels before the mystery of life and says, "Teach me." Humility invites us to hold our beliefs lightly, not because they aren't deeply cherished, but because we know there is always more to discover. It creates space for new perspectives and deeper wisdom. Instead of clinging to rigid conclusions, the humble heart is willing to be challenged, stretched, and changed. This kind of humility also nurtures more authentic relationships—with God, with ourselves, and with others. When we stop pretending we have all the answers or that we must appear perfect, we can begin to live more honestly. We make peace with our imperfections. We stop judging others so harshly. And we discover the gentle strength that comes from grace. In contrast, Religion often fosters pride masquerading as certainty. It exalts having the "right" answers over asking the right questions, and in doing so, can stunt spiritual growth. Pride closes the door to transformation, while humility holds it open.

Big Faith, by contrast, values humility as a posture of lifelong learning. It honours the journey rather than the arrival, and it trusts that truth unfolds over time. It makes room for reverence, for awe, and for the kind of wonder that keeps our faith vibrant. As Kierkegaard put it, *"Humility is not a virtue that can be acquired once and for all; it is a continuous process of learning and growth."* (Kierkegaard, 1843) [9] And in that process, we are changed—not just in what we believe, but in how we live, how we love, and how we see the world.

CHAPTER 5

THE QUIET POWER OF LITTLE FAITH

HOW LITTLE FAITH CAN ACHIEVE GREAT THINGS:
THE POWER OF SMALL BEGINNINGS

How Small Steps Become Great Exploits

The idea that Little Faith can lead to great things may seem counterintuitive in a world that celebrates spectacle. But history, psychology, scripture, and experience all tell another story: that greatness is often born in quiet beginnings, in steady steps, in whispered yeses when no one else is watching.

Transformation rarely announces itself with fireworks. It begins, more often than not, with a moment of courage, a choice to believe again, or a single act of kindness. Little Faith is not about size or scale—it's about substance. It doesn't require thunderous declarations or dramatic leaps. Instead, it thrives in simplicity and consistency. As the Bible reminds us,

"Faith is the substance of things hoped for, the evidence of things not yet seen." (Hebrews 11:1)

The Tipping Point: When Small Actions Shift Everything

As Malcolm Gladwell writes, *"The tipping point is that magic moment when an idea, trend, or social behaviour crosses a threshold, tips, and spreads like wildfire."* (Gladwell, 2000) [1] That moment rarely arrives with warning—but it is always preceded by small, repeated acts. A single conversation can spark a movement. A quiet prayer can shift an entire heart. A daily choice to forgive can reshape generations. Little Faith honours these beginnings. It recognises the power of the seed before the tree. It whispers that hope matters—even when there is no visible harvest. It reminds us that impact is not always immediate, but often exponential.

Overcoming Fear: Building Confidence One Step at a Time

Fear and doubt often stand at the door of transformation. But Little Faith doesn't need all the answers before moving forward. It just needs one step. Psychologist Albert Bandura called this *self-efficacy*—*"the belief in one's ability to succeed in specific situations or accomplish a task"* (Bandura, 1997) [2]. This belief grows not from grand affirmations, but from small wins. Each courageous decision, however minor, builds our confidence. Getting out of bed on a hard day. Trying again after rejection. Apologising when it hurts. These actions whisper, *you're still in this.* You're still moving.

Little Faith gives us agency. It helps us focus on the next step—not the entire staircase. And over time, those steps become strength. They build a quiet resilience that fear cannot shake. As Bandura reminds us, *"Self-efficacy is not a fixed trait, but a dynamic and changing process that can be developed and strengthened over time."* (Bandura, 1997) [2]

The Flywheel Effect: Small Efforts, Massive Momentum

Author Jim Collins describes this phenomenon in his book *Good to Great*: *"The flywheel effect is a concept that describes how a small, consistent effort can build momentum and lead to significant results over time."* (Collins, 2001) [3] Imagine pushing a heavy wheel. At first, nothing happens. Then, slowly, a shift. With every push, momentum builds. Eventually, the wheel turns on its own—powered by all the small, invisible effort that came before. This applies in every arena—business, activism, relationships, inner growth. One thoughtful email. One repeated apology. One creative risk. One kind response. Over time, they compound. They shape culture, heal families, and transform hearts.

Big Faith, when misunderstood, sometimes demands instant change. But Little Faith understands process. It doesn't rush results. It values showing up, again and again, even when no one claps.

The Compound Effect: Faithfulness Over Flash

Darren Hardy calls this the compound effect—*"the principle that small, consistent actions can lead to significant results over time."* (Hardy, 2010) [4] Whether saving a little each day or choosing a daily moment of prayer, the long-term result can be profound.

In spiritual life, five minutes of reflection, a quiet morning prayer, or a daily act of gratitude can shape a soul. These choices may seem small in the moment—but like drops of water, they wear down stone and carve out rivers. Over time, they transform the landscape.

Little Faith invites us to trust the process. To believe that hidden consistency is more powerful than dramatic displays. That slow growth is still growth. That obedience in secret is not wasted.

A Quiet Yes Can Change Everything

The world may celebrate grand gestures, but the kingdom of God often begins with the smallest seed. One whispered yes. One open hand. One decision to try again. As Gladwell reminds us, *"The smallest action can have a profound impact, and the largest actions can have little or no impact at all."* (Gladwell, 2000) [1] True faith is not proven by its volume but by its endurance. And Little Faith, quietly lived and faithfully repeated, is more powerful than we know.

Building Habits: The Foundation of Spiritual Growth and Big Faith

Building positive habits and daily rhythms is foundational to spiritual growth and the development of Big Faith. When we establish consistent practices, we begin to shape not only our routines but also our identity—cultivating a deeper sense of connection to God and to our own inner life (Duhigg, 2012) [5]. Habits have the power to direct our thoughts, shape our responses, and over time, transform our lives. As Charles Duhigg explains, ***"Habits are automatic behaviours that can be changed by understanding the cue-routine-reward loop."*** (Duhigg, 2012) [5] This means habits aren't fixed—they're fluid. By recognising what triggers a certain behaviour (the cue), what we do in response (the routine), and what we gain from it (the reward), we can consciously replace harmful patterns with life-giving ones. In the spiritual context, this might look like creating space for prayer each morning, reading scripture before bed, or building a habit of serving others regularly. These daily or weekly rhythms may feel small, but they are powerful. Over time, they root us. They draw us closer to the divine. They reinforce what matters most.

Importantly, building healthy habits can also help us overcome inner resistance and external pressure. In seasons of emotional difficulty or spiritual dryness, routine becomes anchor. It keeps us grounded when inspiration fades. And with each consistent act of devotion—no matter how ordinary—we plant seeds that grow in faith, maturity, and inner strength.

Big Faith is not sustained by big feelings—it's sustained by meaningful, repeated action.

As Duhigg reminds us, *"Habits are a key part of how we change and grow, and understanding how habits work can help us make better choices and live more fulfilling lives."* (Duhigg, 2012) [5] In other words, faith flourishes where habits hold.

Celebrate Small Wins: The Power of Progress and Momentum

Celebrating small wins is more than a motivational tactic—it is a spiritual discipline. In the journey of faith, progress isn't always loud or visible. That's why recognising even the smallest victories is essential. Every small step forward reinforces momentum and helps us remain rooted in joy, hope, and perseverance (Amabile, 1988) [6]. Psychologist Teresa Amabile describes this as the progress principle: *"The progress principle is the idea that small wins can have a profound impact on motivation and creativity."* (Amabile, 1988) [6] When we pause to acknowledge progress—even if it's just a single day of consistency—we reinforce our sense of purpose and remind ourselves that transformation is happening. In spiritual growth and Big Faith this might mean celebrating the fact that we prayed this morning, showed up for worship, forgave someone, or kept a commitment to serve. These moments may seem minor in isolation, but together they form a trail of evidence—proof that we're growing, becoming, deepening.

Celebrating small wins also helps us keep going when the journey feels slow or unclear. It builds resilience. It affirms that progress is being made even when the results are not immediate or dramatic. When we train ourselves to see and honour the little moments of faithfulness, we shift our mindset from striving to gratitude.

In contrast, an overemphasis on Big Faith can sometimes lead to unrealistic expectations, where only the grand gestures feel worthy of celebration. This can leave us discouraged or disconnected from the quieter, steadier rhythms that truly shape us. But Little Faith—and the consistent discipline it nurtures—reminds us that every step matters.

Celebrating small wins allows us to savour the journey.

As Amabile notes, *"The progress principle is a powerful tool for maintaining motivation and creativity, and for achieving success in all areas of life."* (Amabile, 1988) [6] And in faith, that success isn't measured by the size of our leap, but by the quiet courage to take the next step.

3. Practicing Big Faith in Small Ways: Everyday Opportunities and Micro-Practices

Everyday opportunities to practise Big Faith are all around us—in our relationships, our work, and how we serve our communities. Faith is not reserved for Sunday mornings; it is meant to be woven into every part of life. When we begin to see our daily decisions as sacred, we start living with deeper intention and connection (Palmer, 2004) [7].

As Parker Palmer reflects, *"The spiritual life is lived in the midst of the ordinary."* (Palmer, 2004) [7] In other words, faith is not about striving— it's about trusting that we are already held. From that place of trust, we begin to live differently. We forgive more freely. We serve more joyfully. We rest more peacefully. Faith doesn't need a platform or spotlight. It lives in how we listen to a friend, how we show kindness to a stranger, or how we carry out a task with integrity. These moments may be small, but they are powerful expressions of belief. One way to strengthen this kind of everyday faith is through micro-practices—small, consistent actions that deepen our spiritual awareness. Whether it's pausing for a breath, expressing gratitude, or whispering a prayer, these practices become anchors in the midst of daily noise (Chopra, 2000) [8].

As Deepak Chopra puts it, *"Every experience of love, beauty, truth, or insight can lead us into the presence of the divine."*-(Chopra, 2000) [8] These moments aren't reserved for sacred spaces—they meet us in the everyday when we open our hearts to notice. Incorporating micro-practices doesn't require hours of spare time. It simply asks for consistency and attention. These small actions can reduce stress, increase clarity, and nurture resilience. They train us to be more present, more hopeful, and more grounded—even when life is uncertain. Ultimately, practising Big Faith in small ways, that is Big Faith Little Religion, is about shifting how we live, not just what we believe. It invites us to bring our faith into the fabric of everyday life—not perfectly, but consistently—with humility, gratitude, and intention.

Integrating Faith into Daily Life

For faith to grow strong and remain sustainable, it must be integrated into our daily routines—not separated into compartments. When faith becomes part of how we think, speak, work, and rest, it moves from belief into embodiment (Tillich, 1957) [9]. As Paul Tillich once said, **"Faith is the courage to accept acceptance."** (Tillich, 1957) [9] In other words, faith is not about striving—it's about trusting that we are already held. From that place of trust, we begin to live differently. We forgive more freely. We serve more joyfully. We rest more peacefully. By making space for spiritual practices throughout the day—moments of stillness, reminders of purpose, or acts of service—we slowly form a lifestyle of faith. One that doesn't depend on performance but flows from presence.

4. Building Momentum for Great Miracles: Creating a Support Network

Great miracles often begin with something small—but they are rarely sustained in isolation. To build real momentum, we need others. A supportive environment is essential for nurturing Big Faith and staying anchored in purpose. When we are surrounded by people who uplift, encourage, and challenge us to believe for more, we find the strength to keep going—especially when things get hard (Cohen, 2004) [10]. Psychologist Sheldon Cohen reminds us, *"Social support is a critical factor in maintaining physical and mental health."* (Cohen, 2004) [10] Beyond physical wellness, this truth extends into spiritual life. When we feel seen, held, and cheered on, we become more resilient. We push through resistance. We step out more boldly. In the context of Big Faith, a strong support network becomes sacred ground. It fosters belonging and spiritual connection. It reminds us that we're not walking alone. When we gather with people who share our convictions—who also believe that the impossible is possible—we are strengthened. Their faith stirs ours. Support networks also create space for honesty. In seasons of fear or doubt, community offers a safe place to be real. Through prayer, encouragement, and shared wisdom, we find courage to keep believing—even when the outcome isn't yet clear. A text message, a coffee conversation, a prayer whispered on someone else's behalf—these small acts carry great power.

Big Faith is not about heroic isolation. It's about intentional connection. It grows best in the soil of community—where grace, accountability, and encouragement flow freely.

Building momentum for great miracles means building a circle that lifts, steadies, and reminds you who you are.

With the right people around you, faith becomes more than belief—it becomes movement. As Cohen reflects, *"Social support is a powerful tool that can help individuals achieve their goals and overcome challenges."* (Cohen, 2004) [10]

Embracing Challenges: Opportunities for Growth and Spiritual Development

Challenges are not interruptions to the journey—they *are* the journey. Rather than viewing hardship as something to avoid or overcome quickly, Little Faith Great Miracles invites us to see challenges as teachers. When we embrace difficulties with openness and courage, we grow stronger in spirit, deeper in faith, and clearer in purpose (Frankl, 1946) [11]. Viktor Frankl wrote extensively on the power of meaning in suffering. He once reflected, *"In some ways, suffering ceases to be suffering at the moment it finds a meaning."* (Frankl, 1946) [11] This reminds us that growth is not born in comfort—it often emerges from pain, from persistence, from learning to hope again after disappointment.

In the context of Big Faith, challenges become more than obstacles—they become invitations. Invitations to trust God when nothing makes sense. Invitations to discover inner strength we didn't know we had. Invitations to become who we were always meant to be. Through hardship, we develop resilience, patience, and perseverance. We learn to rely on God more than ourselves. We begin to understand that real transformation doesn't happen in the absence of pressure, but through it. Our values become clearer. We begin to act from a place of intention rather than reaction. In this way, the very things that seem to stand in our way become the pathway forward.

It is not the absence of struggle that marks a life of Big Faith—but the decision to face struggle with meaning, trust, and surrender.

Staying Focused and Motivated: Maintaining Momentum on the Path to Great Miracles

Great Miracles are not always born in a single moment—they are built in the daily decisions to keep going. Momentum is sustained not just through inspiration, but through focus, self-care, and community. Staying motivated requires us to nourish our minds, bodies, and spirits with intention and love (Duckworth, 2016) [12]. Psychologist Angela Duckworth, author of *Grit*, notes, **"*Enthusiasm is common. Endurance is rare.*"** (Duckworth, 2016) [12] This highlights a vital truth: it's easy to start strong, but staying the course takes discipline. It takes heart. It takes the quiet strength to keep showing up—even when results are slow or setbacks arise. Celebrating small wins is one way to maintain this endurance. Recognising progress—however minor—fuels motivation. Whether it's finishing a journal entry, praying through a hard day, or keeping a promise to yourself, these victories deserve honour. They remind us that we *are* moving forward, even if the pace feels slow. Self-care is equally essential.

We cannot pour from an empty cup. Tending to our emotional, physical, and spiritual needs allows us to stay energised and aligned. Whether it's a walk, a nap, a moment of stillness, or connection with nature, these acts restore us so we can keep going.

And finally, staying connected to others who believe in us—and in our vision—strengthens our resolve. When we are tired or disheartened, the voice of a friend, mentor, or community can reignite our flame. Encouragement, accountability, and prayer become vital fuel on the journey.

In the end, staying focused and motivated is about finding rhythm—not perfection. It's about allowing grace to carry us when strength runs low, and letting faith steady us through the long middle. But with Little Faith Great Miracles, we learn to endure—and to flourish.

Overcoming Obstacles: Achieving Great Miracles through Resilience and Perseverance

Every journey of Big Faith encounters resistance. Obstacles aren't a sign that we're on the wrong path—they're often confirmation that we're on a meaningful one. The pursuit of great miracles demands more than just vision. It requires grit, grace, and a willingness to grow through what we go through. Psychologist Carol Dweck, author of *Mindset*, describes a growth mindset as *"the belief that abilities and intelligence can be developed through hard work, dedication, and persistence."* (Dweck, 2006) [12]. This perspective changes everything. Instead of seeing setbacks as signals to stop, we begin to see them as stepping stones. Failure becomes feedback. Delay becomes preparation. Obstacles become teachers. Developing this kind of mindset allows us to meet difficulty with curiosity rather than defeat. We start to ask, *What can this teach me?* rather than *Why is this happening to me?* That shift in perspective cultivates resilience. It fuels perseverance. It empowers us to keep going, even when the road is steep. But we don't walk this road alone. A support network is essential in moments of struggle. Whether it's a mentor offering wisdom, a friend reminding us of our strength, or a community praying us through, the presence of others helps lighten the load. Encouragement and accountability are not luxuries—they are necessities. Equally important is the practice of self-compassion. When progress feels slow or failure stings, we must remember to treat ourselves with kindness. Not everything will go according to plan. But setbacks do not define us. Grace is not just something we extend to others—it's something we must extend to ourselves.

Overcoming obstacles on the path to Great Miracles is not about avoiding hardship. It's about growing through it. It's about choosing faith over fear, courage over comfort, and hope over helplessness.

As Dweck writes, *"A growth mindset is not just a way of thinking, but a way of being that can help individuals achieve their full potential."* (Dweck, 2006) [13]

Sustaining Momentum: Consistency, Adaptation, and Continuous Growth

We've explored before how momentum is something we build—through intention, repetition, and consistency. But it bears repeating: once that momentum is in motion, it must be sustained. It takes ongoing effort, clarity of purpose, and a heart that is open to growth. The path to great miracles is rarely fast or linear. It moves through rhythm—through steady alignment, flexibility, and the courage to keep showing up. As previously mentioned, Jim Collins' concept of the *flywheel effect* captures this beautifully. Progress often begins slowly, each small push adding to the wheel's motion. At first, it may feel like nothing is shifting. But with faithful effort, the turning gains pace. What starts as effort eventually becomes momentum. And that momentum, once formed, is best maintained not through force—but through rhythm. Yet even the most consistent rhythm can stall if we're unwilling to adapt. Circumstances change. Seasons shift. What worked yesterday may need refining today. Growth requires flexibility—a willingness to adjust course without losing direction. This is not a sign of weakness but wisdom. The ability to adapt ensures that we remain responsive, not reactive, anchored in vision but open in execution. Psychologist Angela Duckworth, known for her work on perseverance and grit, reminds us: *"Enthusiasm is common. Endurance is rare."* (Duckworth, 2016) [13]. That endurance—the quiet resilience to keep going when the initial excitement has faded—is what sustains momentum. It's built not only through discipline but through vision, purpose, and the daily practice of showing up. Celebrating progress plays a vital role in this process. Small wins remind us that we are moving forward. They energise us. They validate the effort. And they build the kind of emotional fuel that keeps the fire burning during slow or silent seasons. Celebration is not indulgence—it's nourishment for the soul of the journey.

Finally, sustaining momentum means remaining a student of your own life. Continuous growth demands curiosity. It invites us to ask questions, seek feedback, and challenge the comfort of plateau. It's not about restlessness, but about remaining awake to the possibilities of becoming more—more aligned, more faithful, more fruitful.

Momentum is not just about moving fast. It's about moving faithfully. With focus, with grace, and with the conviction that great miracles are often the fruit of quiet perseverance over time.

CHAPTER 6

REVOLUTIONIZING YOUR WORLD

The Impact of Big Faith on Your Community: A Ripple Effect

Big Faith doesn't just change the individual—it changes the world around them. When lived authentically and courageously, it can create a ripple effect, inspiring others and sparking tangible transformation across families, communities, and even nations. This isn't just poetic language—it's a reality grounded in both history and human psychology. As psychologist Herbert Kelman observed, *"The process of social influence is a complex one, involving both cognitive and motivational factors."* (Kelman, 1961) [1] In other words, change doesn't happen by sheer logic or emotion alone. It's the deep resonance of both heart and mind that moves people to act. When someone walks in Big Faith—with conviction and compassion—they don't have to preach. Their life becomes an invitation. Their courage becomes contagious. We've seen this ripple effect play out countless times. One person's bold act of faith can shift the atmosphere around them. A woman opens her home to mentor young girls, and before long, an entire network of support grows. A man chooses integrity in the workplace, and suddenly others feel empowered to do the same. A student speaks up for justice on campus, and it plants a seed that grows into a movement. These moments rarely feel "big" at first—but over time, they multiply and inspire, just like ripples on water. This phenomenon is especially visible in the context of social justice. The Civil Rights Movement in the United States offers a powerful case study. It wasn't just a political uprising—it was a movement grounded in Big Faith. Figures like Dr Martin Luther King Jr. demonstrated how faith, when lived out through nonviolence and moral conviction, could shake systems of oppression and bring about lasting change.

As historian Taylor Branch puts it, *"The Civil Rights Movement was a testament to the power of faith and nonviolent resistance in bringing about social change."* (Branch, 1988) [2] Dr King's faith didn't stay behind a pulpit—it marched in the streets, crossed bridges, and stood before injustice with unwavering courage. His example shows us that when Big Faith is harnessed for the common good, it has the power to reform not only individuals, but entire nations. The ripple effect of Big Faith is not reserved for history books or global figures. It begins in kitchens and classrooms, boardrooms and bus stops. It starts with small acts of integrity, love, and boldness that speak louder than any sermon. And as more people catch that vision—of a life surrendered, purposeful, and brave—those ripples gather into waves. Together, they begin to reshape what's possible.

Empowering Others: Creating a Multiplier Effect through Big Faith

Big Faith multiplies when it empowers. It doesn't stop at personal transformation—it ignites change in others. Those who walk in Big Faith

Little Religion, often find themselves naturally becoming catalysts for growth, not because they strive to lead, but because their lives inspire others to rise. Empowerment is one of the most powerful fruits of Big Faith. It begins when we stop trying to impress and start seeking to impact. Whether it's mentoring a young person, offering encouragement to someone in transition, or giving someone the tools to pursue their calling, Big Faith equips others to believe that change is possible—and that they are part of that change.

As leadership thinker John C. Maxwell puts it, *"Leaders become great not because of their power, but because of their ability to empower others." (Maxwell, 2005) [3]* That's what Big Faith does—it releases possibility into others. When people see someone walking confidently in their purpose, they are more likely to explore their own.

Empowering others can take the form of teaching, listening, praying, resourcing, or simply showing up consistently. It's not just about helping people succeed—it's about helping them believe they can. This multiplier effect has a ripple far wider than we can measure. As one person becomes empowered, they go on to empower others, and the wave of transformation grows. Big Faith Little Religion creates a network of influence—not through hierarchy, but through humility and hope.

True empowerment isn't controlling or prescriptive. It's invitational. It says, *You too can rise. You too are called. You too are capable.* And in that shared belief, lives begin to change—one act of faith at a time. As Bandura notes, *"Empowering others is a powerful way to create positive change, as it enables individuals to take control of their own lives and become agents of their own destiny."* (Bandura, 1997) [4]

Creating Positive Change with Little Religion: Breaking Free from Dogma

When faith becomes too rigid, it stops moving. And when it stops moving, it stops transforming lives. That's where Little Religion offers a refreshing alternative—a way of approaching spirituality that is light, liberating, and deeply rooted in personal connection with the divine. Big Faith Little Religion doesn't ask for performance. It invites participation. It's not built on strict creeds or institutional structures, but on lived experience—on moments of love, justice, truth, and grace that reveal God in the everyday. Karen Armstrong has long championed this approach. In her reflections, she explains that Little Religion "allows for a more nuanced and contextualised understanding of faith," one that invites curiosity and compassion over certainty and control (Armstrong, 2009) [4].

This isn't about being anti-religious. It's about loosening the grip of dogma so faith can breathe again. Little Religion asks: *What brings healing? What fosters love? What leads us closer to justice and wholeness?* And then it follows those questions—not to dismantle faith, but to deepen it.

People drawn to Little Religion are often those who have been bruised by the weight of systems or silenced by rigid orthodoxy. They're not faithless—they're hungry for something real. And when given permission to explore, many find a stronger, more meaningful connection with God than ever before.

Practical Application

We don't have to look far to see Big Faith Little Religion at work. Across the world, movements of care, justice, and compassion are often led by people of deep, simple faith—people who may never quote scripture but embody its message.

The *Little Sisters of the Poor*, for example, have lived out this kind of quiet, transformative spirituality. Without fanfare or platform, they have cared for the vulnerable with dignity and love. Researcher Kathleen Kane notes, *"The Little Sisters of the Poor embody the principles of Little Religion, demonstrating the transformative power of faith in action."* (Kane, 2013) [5] These acts of service may not make headlines, but they change lives. They are expressions of a faith that is not loud—but deeply alive.

Big Faith Little Religion doesn't need titles or pulpits. It needs open hearts and willing hands. Its power lies in its simplicity—in doing the next faithful thing, again and again. And when enough people do that, the world begins to change.

Innovative Solutions: Harnessing the Creative Potential of Big Faith Little Religion

Big Faith Little Religion can foster innovative solutions to complex problems, unencumbered by traditional thinking. By embracing a more flexible and adaptive approach to faith, individuals can tap into the creative potential of Big Faith Little Religion (Florida, 2002) [6]. This approach recognises that traditional frameworks can often be limiting, preventing individuals from exploring new solutions to today's challenges.

As economist **Richard Florida** notes, *"The most innovative solutions often arise from the intersection of different disciplines and perspectives."* (Florida, 2002) [6] This insight underscores the value of open-mindedness, creativity, and cross-disciplinary thinking. Big Faith

Little Religion invites this kind of freedom—encouraging exploration, experimentation, and new connections that lead to fresh approaches. By moving away from rigid structures and embracing a more personalised spiritual lens, individuals can unlock their own creative capacity. Big Faith Little Religion allows space for questions, new interpretations, and non-linear pathways to emerge—often leading to breakthrough thinking.

This freedom also fosters courage. When there's no pressure to conform to fixed doctrines, there's greater room to imagine, risk, and try again. The result is not just spiritual growth, but innovation that has practical impact—solutions that are spiritually grounded, emotionally intelligent, and socially responsive.

"Innovation is the key to unlocking human potential and creating a better future." (Florida, 2002) [6]

Inspiring Others to Join the Revolution: Leading by Example

Leading by example is essential in demonstrating the power of Big Faith Little Religion. By embodying the principles of these approaches, individuals can inspire others to join the movement. This approach recognises that people are more likely to be influenced by authentic action than persuasive rhetoric. As change strategist **John Kotter** observes, *"People change what they do less because they are given analysis than because they are shown a truth that influences their feelings."* (Kotter, 1996) [7] This insight emphasises the emotional and relational power of lived example.

When others *see* transformation—rather than simply *hear* about it—they are more inclined to participate and believe.

Leading by example requires deep integrity and ongoing commitment. It involves embodying values like courage, humility, and compassion—not in lofty theory, but in the details of everyday life. When faith becomes visible in action, it invites others to explore it for themselves. Sharing one's journey also plays a role. Vulnerability, honesty, and testimony create resonance. When someone opens up about their spiritual process—its doubts, turns, and triumphs—it gives permission for others to begin their own.

Change spreads through authenticity.

When individuals live out the principles of Big Faith, Little Religion with conviction and care, they create the conditions for others to follow—not through pressure, but through presence. As Kotter puts it, *"Transformation happens when the heart is engaged before the head is convinced."* (Kotter, 1996) [7]

The Power of Storytelling: Inspiring Others to Join the Revolution

Storytelling is one of the most powerful tools we have for inspiring others. It moves beyond explanation and reaches into emotion, illustrating the transformative power of Big Faith Little Religion through real, human experiences. When individuals share their own stories, they foster connection, create community, and invite others into the revolution (Denning, 2005) [8]. As Stephen Denning writes, *"Storytelling is a powerful tool for inspiring and motivating others, creating a sense of shared purpose and meaning.*" (Denning, 2005) [8] This shared purpose is essential. It is not just about passing on information—it's about awakening something within the listener. When people hear a story that mirrors their struggle, their hopes, or their longings, they begin to imagine that transformation is possible for them too. The beauty of storytelling lies in its simplicity. A personal anecdote can convey more depth than a doctrine. It brings Big Faith to life, not as an abstract concept, but as a lived, breathing journey. Through honest and vulnerable storytelling, barriers come down, empathy is born, and the revolution grows stronger.

Even more, when we tell the stories of others—those who've walked in Big Faith Little Religion and seen lives changed—we extend that circle of impact. These stories act as echoes of possibility, showing that transformation is not just theoretical. It's happening. It's real. It can happen again.

Facts may inform, but stories ignite. In a world saturated with information, it is story that still captures the heart. And when the heart is captured, the journey of transformation begins.

Building a Movement: Creating a Community of Like-Minded Individuals for Big Faith Little Religion

Movements are not built in isolation—they begin with shared conviction and grow through collective momentum. The heart of Big Faith Little Religion beats strongest in community. To build something that lasts, we must create spaces where like-minded individuals can gather, connect, and collaborate. These communities become the soil where transformation takes root and spreads. As marketing thinker Philip Kotler observes, *"Building a movement requires a clear sense of purpose, a compelling vision, and a supportive community."* (Kotler, 2002) [9] When people gather around a vision that resonates deeply, they begin to see themselves not just as followers, but as co-creators of change. A movement is born when isolated beliefs become a collective voice.

Big Faith and Little Religion are not in opposition. They complement each other—one offering depth and personal conviction, the other offering freedom and flexibility. Together, they call us to live authentically and courageously, rooted in something bigger than ourselves, yet free from the need to perform for approval.

This movement envisions a world where faith is lived out—not just preached. Where justice and compassion are more than ideals, but shared practices. Where spiritual growth doesn't demand conformity, but invites creativity, honesty, and boldness.

To join the movement is to step into a story that's still being written. It's to show up—heart open, faith alive, willing to learn and ready to lead. Within this community, individuals share stories, sharpen vision, organise initiatives, and stir change. It's not about uniformity, but unity—a collective hunger to live with deeper meaning and greater love.

Big Faith, Little Religion is not just a concept—it's a call.

A call to rise, to gather, and to create a new way forward. One that welcomes questions, honours truth, and builds a world that reflects grace, justice, and joy.

As Kotler notes, "*Building a movement is not just about achieving a goal - it's about creating a sense of community and shared purpose that can inspire and mobilize others.*" (Kotler, 2002) [9]

Overcoming Obstacles: Strategies for Success

Revolutionizing your world will not be without its challenges. Along the way, you will encounter obstacles—both internal and external—that test your resolve and vision. Among the most common and paralysing is fear, often accompanied by self-doubt. These inner saboteurs can hold you back, making you question your worth or capacity. But they are not immovable. One of the most effective ways to confront fear and self-doubt is by strengthening your belief in your own ability—what psychologist Albert Bandura termed *self-efficacy*. Building self-efficacy involves breaking your goals into smaller, achievable steps and acknowledging progress along the way (Bandura, 1997) [1]. Each success, no matter how small, reinforces your confidence and reshapes your self-image into one rooted in courage and capability.

You may also face resistance from others—those who dismiss your ideas, question your direction, or actively undermine your efforts. This kind of opposition can be disheartening, but it can also be navigated. Robert Cialdini, a leading voice in the science of influence, emphasises the power of relationship-building and persuasive communication. Techniques such as storytelling, active listening, and establishing common ground can dissolve resistance and build unexpected alliances (Cialdini, 2009) [2].

Another hurdle may be the lack of resources—limited time, money, or access to people who can help you realise your vision. These constraints are real, but not final. As Richard Florida notes, innovation thrives at the intersection of creativity and necessity (Florida, 2002) [3]. By thinking laterally, forming strategic partnerships, seeking unconventional funding sources, or reimagining how goals can be achieved, you can often accomplish more with less.

Sustaining Momentum: Strategies for Staying Focused and Committed

Starting strong is one thing. Staying the course is another. Sustaining momentum is about more than just motivation—it's about creating structure, community, and flexibility.

One key strategy is to set clear and specific goals. Research by Locke and Latham has shown that well-defined objectives, broken down into manageable steps, fuel motivation and keep efforts aligned (Locke & Latham, 2002) [4]. Milestones matter. Celebrating them—even quietly— helps you see how far you've come and renews your focus.

Another critical factor is community. Surrounding yourself with people who share your values and commitment creates a powerful support system. Whether it's peers, mentors, or close friends, these relationships become sources of encouragement, accountability, and inspiration (Cohen, 2004) [5]. They remind you that you're not in this alone.

Finally, sustaining momentum requires a posture of adaptability. No path to change is linear. As Peter Senge argues, lasting growth comes from systems that learn and evolve (Senge, 1990) [6]. Being open to new insights, willing to adjust your approach, and able to respond to unexpected shifts is what allows your vision to endure and expand.

With these strategies—anchored in self-efficacy, influence, creativity, structure, support, and adaptability—you can move through obstacles and keep your movement alive. Not by rushing, but by rising—step by step, consistently and courageously.

CHAPTER 7

THE POWER OF LITTLE RELIGION

1. Breaking Free from the Shackles of Traditional Religion

Traditional religion can stifle personal growth, creativity, and freedom by imposing rigid structures, dogma, and expectations (Fromm, 1950) [1]. This often results in a sense of suffocation, where individuals feel constrained by the rules and requirements of their faith. As psychologist Erich Fromm observed, *"To be fully human, one must reclaim the courage to think and act independently of authoritarian structures."* (Fromm, 1950) [1] This highlights how traditional religion, when built on external authority rather than internal transformation, can hinder true freedom and creative expression.

Recognising the constraints of traditional religion is the first step towards breaking free from its grip. This demands a willingness to question inherited structures and challenge what no longer serves personal or spiritual growth. When individuals become aware of how rigid religious systems limit creativity and exploration, they begin to open up to more liberating expressions of faith.

One of the main limitations of traditional religion lies in its overemphasis on dogma and doctrine. This rigid allegiance to fixed beliefs often silences curiosity, discourages doubt, and suppresses innovation. In contrast, *Little Religion* embraces the fluidity of personal experience and the richness of spiritual discovery. It opens the door for individuals to shape their faith through lived insight rather than imposed belief. Also, traditional religion tends to enforce institutional frameworks that dictate how faith should look, feel, and function. These systems can leave people feeling alienated from their true selves, forced to perform rather than participate. *Little Religion*, on the other hand, honours individuality. It invites people to craft a spirituality that resonates deeply with their values and voice.

Breaking free from the shackles of traditional religion doesn't mean discarding faith altogether—it means reclaiming it. It means choosing authenticity over performance, freedom over fear and relationship over ritual. As Fromm writes, ***"The only way to achieve true freedom is to break free from the constraints of traditional authority."*** (Fromm, 1950) [1] It is this journey—from obedience to ownership—that marks the beginning of transformative, life-giving faith.

Challenging Authority: Cultivating Critical Thinking and Exploration

Challenging authority, doctrine, and dogma is a defining feature of *Big Faith Little Religion*. It invites readers to question long-held assumptions and inherited traditions, promoting a spirituality that is alive, thoughtful, and evolving (Armstrong, 2009) [2]. This approach recognises that blind acceptance can limit personal growth and hinder genuine spiritual development. In contrast, *Big Faith Little Religion* affirms the value of critical thinking as a spiritual discipline—one that deepens our understanding of both ourselves and the sacred. As religious scholar Karen Armstrong notes, *"When religion ceases to be about compassion and becomes about control, it loses its power to transform."* (Armstrong, 2009) [2] This reminds us that authentic spirituality must prioritise inner transformation over external compliance. Critical reflection becomes a necessary practice—allowing us to differentiate between what nurtures the soul and what merely enforces conformity.

Challenging authority also involves turning the spotlight inward. It asks us to question our own assumptions, cultural conditioning, and unconscious biases. This kind of inner honesty can be uncomfortable—but it is essential. Without it, spirituality risks becoming performance rather than encounter. By promoting thoughtful examination over passive acceptance, *Big Faith Little Religion* empowers individuals to reclaim their agency and shape a spiritual path that is personal, grounded, and authentic.

Embracing Personal Autonomy: Taking Ownership of One's Spiritual Journey

Embracing personal autonomy is central to the spirit of *Big Faith Little Religion*. It encourages individuals to take ownership of their spiritual journey by making choices that reflect their values, lived experience, and deepest convictions (Maslow, 1962) [3]. This approach honours the uniqueness of each person's path, recognising that spirituality is not one-size-fits-all. What leads one person to freedom may not speak to another—and that's not only acceptable, it's sacred. As psychologist Abraham Maslow notes, *"Self-actualising people have the courage to listen to their own voices, even when they contradict the crowd."* (Maslow, 1962) [3] This insight speaks directly to the heart of *Big Faith, Little Religion*—that spiritual maturity emerges when we tune into our own soul and trust its direction, even when it challenges the norms around us.

Taking ownership of one's journey also means moving beyond passive consumption of doctrine. It involves seeking out new ideas, exploring unfamiliar paths, asking hard questions, and integrating what feels true. This kind of engagement builds a faith that is not only deeply personal, but also enduring. Instead of leaning on external approval, individuals begin to draw from an internal well of wisdom—one shaped by curiosity, honesty, and love.

In doing so, *Big Faith Little Religion* becomes more than a departure from tradition. It becomes a return to self, to God, and to the sacred mystery that calls each person by name.

2. Finding Freedom in Little Religion: Liberty from Dogma

Little Religion offers a profound and personal kind of freedom— freedom from the heavy weight of rigid dogma and freedom to explore spirituality in a way that is honest, evolving and deeply alive (Tillich, 1957) [4]. Traditional religious systems often emphasise strict doctrines that can leave little room for individual thought or spiritual nuance. In contrast, *Little Religion* invites us into a space where our questions are welcome, our experiences matter, and our doubts are not disqualifying. As theologian Paul Tillich wrote, **"The Protestant principle is the principle of freedom—the freedom to question and to seek."** (Tillich, 1957) [4] That freedom is not rebellion for its own sake. It is the sacred permission to think, to wonder, and to stretch our understanding of God beyond the confines of inherited formulas. But this liberation isn't only about external authority. It's also an invitation to loosen our grip on the internal scripts we've absorbed—those silent expectations that say we must always be certain, always be right, always be in control. *Little Religion* asks us to soften those inner certainties, making space for curiosity, self-compassion, and growth.

Embracing Uncertainty: The Beauty of Ambiguity

A defining mark of *Big Faith Little Religion* is its comfort with mystery. Rather than clinging to black-and-white answers, it encourages us to sit within the grey—to listen, to reflect, and to hold paradox with open hands (Palmer, 2004) [5]. Spiritual growth is not a straight line; it is a winding path marked by mystery, tension, and surprise. As Parker Palmer reminds us, *"Wholeness does not mean perfection—it means embracing brokenness as an integral part of life."* (Palmer, 2004) [5] This perspective reframes ambiguity as something sacred. It is not a flaw in the spiritual life—it is part of what makes it real. Living with uncertainty requires a kind of holy surrender. We begin to let go of the need to control outcomes or explain everything. We become more open to what is, rather than what should be. In this way, ambiguity becomes not a burden but a portal—leading us deeper into truth, into self-awareness, and into communion with the mystery of God.

Cultivating Inner Peace: Finding Calm in the Midst of Chaos

Big Faith Little Religion fosters not just belief—but being. In the midst of life's turbulence, it offers an anchor: a deep, grounded peace that doesn't depend on external conditions (Chopra, 2000) [6]. This kind of peace is not fleeting. It is a state of soul—born from presence, nourished by reflection and sustained through spiritual openness. As Deepak Chopra writes, *"In the midst of movement and chaos, keep stillness inside of you."* (Chopra, 2000) [6] This speaks to the essence of *Little Religion*: the ability to stay grounded within, even when the world outside is swirling with uncertainty. To cultivate this inner stillness, we must become comfortable with silence. Not the kind of silence that hides our feelings, but the kind that allows space for them. It means pausing before we react. Breathing before we speak. Turning inward, not as a retreat from reality, but as a return to truth.

Practices like meditation, prayer, walking in nature, or even sitting quietly with a cup of tea—these simple rhythms can reawaken our connection to peace. They invite us to listen, not just to the world, but to the still small voice within. This inner peace is not the absence of struggle. It is the presence of clarity and trust amid the unknown. *Big Faith Little Religion* doesn't promise that storms will disappear. But it helps us learn how to breathe within them.

3. Focusing on What Truly Matters

Prioritizing Personal Values

In the pursuit of authentic spiritual growth, we are often called to pause and reflect on what genuinely matters. This journey is not about performing for others or conforming to inherited expectations—it's about returning to the inner compass of our own values. When we begin to identify and prioritise those values, we make space for meaning, purpose, and fulfilment to take root (Rokeach, 1973) [7]. As psychologist Milton Rokeach reminds us, "Values are the core of a person's belief system, influencing their attitudes, behaviours, and decisions." (Rokeach, 1973) [7] In other words, values are not merely preferences— they are the spiritual architecture of a life well lived. Prioritising values means clearing away the clutter. It means examining what we've inherited—whether from religion, culture, or upbringing— and asking: Does this still resonate with who I am and who I'm becoming? It invites a gentle but courageous letting go of expectations that no longer serve, and a reorienting toward what brings life. When we align our spiritual journey with what we truly value—whether it's justice, compassion, creativity, truth, or stillness—we begin to walk a path that is not only personal but powerful. It becomes easier to say no to what distracts and yes to what nourishes. We find ourselves grounded, even in change. Anchored, even in ambiguity.

And in that space, spiritual growth becomes less about striving and more about becoming.

Letting Go of Non-Essentials: Embracing Spiritual Freedom

Spiritual maturity invites us not only to seek what is true—but to release what is no longer necessary. Letting go of non-essential beliefs, practices, or traditions that once served us but now hinder our growth is a profound act of faith. It is here that we begin to embrace spiritual freedom, trusting our inner wisdom rather than chasing external validation (Kierkegaard, 1843) [8]. As Søren Kierkegaard wrote, *"Life can* only be understood backwards; but it must be lived forwards." (Kierkegaard, 1843) [8] His words invite us to reflect deeply on the role of hindsight in spiritual growth, while also reminding us that we must keep moving forward, open to the unknown, untethered from the past. Growth often means releasing what no longer fits—even when we once held it dear.

Letting go, then, is not failure. It is liberation. It is the holy work of discernment—of sifting through what was inherited or adopted and asking: *Is this still leading me deeper into truth, love, and wholeness?* When the answer is no, the invitation is to gently lay it down. This process might involve releasing outdated doctrines that once offered comfort but now feel misaligned. It may mean walking away from rituals that feel hollow or obligations that no longer hold meaning. By loosening our grip on these non-essentials, we make room for the Spirit to do something new.

In that space of surrender, a more authentic and life-giving faith can emerge—one shaped not by fear or pressure, but by presence and trust.

Simplifying Spiritual Practices: Focusing on What Brings Joy

Simplifying spiritual practices by focusing on what brings joy, peace, and fulfilment is essential (Francis de Sales, 1609) [9]. This means releasing unnecessary complexity, embracing simplicity, and trusting your own spiritual instincts. As spiritual teacher Francis de Sales once said, *"The simplest and most direct way to attain spiritual growth is to focus on the present moment."* (Francis de Sales, 1609) [9]. His words serve as a reminder to remain grounded in the here and now, letting go of distraction and excess in order to return to what nourishes the soul.

To simplify is not to abandon depth, but to strip away what no longer serves. Whether it's through meditation, prayer, stillness, or walking in nature, the path becomes clearer when shaped by what brings life and joy. In this way, spiritual practice becomes less about performance and more about presence—a quiet return to what truly matters.

CHAPTER 8

IGNITING REVOLUTION WITH BIG FAITH LITTLE RELIGION

Spark of Great Miracles and the Power of Big Faith Little Religion

Big Faith Little Religion is the spark that ignites revolutions. It fuels passion, provokes purpose, and empowers us to pursue greatness. But it is often **Little Faith**—a simple, humble beginning—that provides the first push forward. It's that first hesitant "yes," that trembling act of courage, that begins to shift everything. Taking the first step, no matter how small, creates movement. It breaks inertia. It stirs belief. And that beginning, though quiet, becomes the seed of something far greater. As leadership coach Rosabeth Moss Kanter observes, *"Everything looks like failure in the middle."* (Kanter, 2006) [1] Her insight reminds us that what begins small is not insignificant—it's foundational. It's the early stage of something transformative. [1]

Building Confidence: The Power of Small Wins

Small wins are not just milestones—they're motivators. Each one creates a ripple effect, reinforcing the belief that progress is possible and that our efforts are not in vain. By noticing, naming, and celebrating small victories, we create momentum. As business thinker Charles Duhigg notes, *"Small wins fuel transformative changes by leveraging tiny advantages into patterns that convince people that bigger achievements are within reach."* (Duhigg, 2012) [2] When individuals celebrate these incremental triumphs, their faith grows stronger, their courage expands, and their vision sharpens.

It's in these micro-moments that Little Faith begins to morph into Big Faith. What began as a whisper turns into a declaration: *I can do this.*

Gradual Progress: The Stepping Stones to Great Miracles

Revolutions are rarely sparked by dramatic leaps. More often, they unfold through steady, faithful steps. Great Miracles are preceded by a thousand small choices—quiet decisions to keep going, to rise again, to believe in what has yet to be seen. As novelist and social critic George Eliot once wrote, *"The strongest principle of growth lies in human choice."* (Eliot, 1871) [3] Growth doesn't just happen—it's built choice by choice, step by step, moment by moment. Each small decision, rooted in faith and sustained by grace, becomes a stepping stone toward transformation.

In the rhythm of Big Faith Little Religion, these steps are sacred. They are not rushed or forced, but steady and honest. They affirm that progress is not measured only by grand gestures, but by consistent, faithful obedience in the ordinary.

Transformative Potential: The Power of Big Faith Little Religion

Big Faith Little Religion carries within it the power to transform. It challenges the status quo, reimagines what is possible, and awakens people to a more vibrant and creative spiritual life. It doesn't simply ask us to believe—it compels us to build, to risk, and to lead with vision. This combination of deep conviction and free-spirited practice gives individuals permission to think differently, question old assumptions, and explore new territory. It encourages courage—the kind that births new ideas and disrupts cycles of stagnation. Big Faith, rooted in passion and purpose, gives rise to Little Religion, which is flexible enough to adapt, respond, and evolve. As philosopher Alfred North Whitehead once observed, *"Religion will not regain its power until it can face change in the same spirit as science."* (Whitehead, 1926) [4] His words remind us that transformation requires openness—a willingness to explore beyond inherited dogma. Through this openness, Big Faith Little Religion becomes a catalyst for innovation, not just in belief, but in action. It sparks revolutions of thought, practice, and community. And as people begin to live out this faith—authentic, adaptive, and alive— they create a ripple effect. That ripple becomes movement. That movement becomes change.

This is the transformative potential of Big Faith Little Religion: not just to inspire individual growth, but to ignite collective awakening—one heart, one community, one bold act at a time.

Unwavering Conviction: The Power of Unshakeable Confidence

Big Faith Little Religion is grounded in a kind of spiritual steadiness—an unwavering conviction that doesn't collapse in the face of adversity. It offers a deep-rooted confidence that enables individuals to keep going, even when the odds are stacked against them. This kind of inner strength isn't loud or performative—it's quiet, steady, and immovable. As civil rights leader Rosa Parks once said, *"You must never be fearful about what you are doing when it is right."* (Parks, 1992) [5] Her words speak to the courage that comes from knowing you're aligned with something greater than yourself. When conviction runs deep, it becomes a compass that guides us through resistance, uncertainty, and difficulty. Unshakeable confidence does not mean arrogance. It means staying rooted when storms come. It means trusting the path even when visibility is low. When people walk in this kind of faith, they don't just survive hardship—they are shaped by it. Their purpose becomes sharper. Their resolve becomes stronger.

Inspiring Others: The Magnetic Effect of Big Faith Little Religion

Big Faith Little Religion doesn't operate in isolation. It radiates. It draws people in. It has a magnetic effect—not because it demands agreement, but because it embodies authenticity and courage. It shows others what is possible when faith is lived freely and boldly. As leadership author Robin Sharma writes, *"Leadership is not about a title or a designation. It's about impact, influence, and inspiration."* (Sharma, 2003) [6] This kind of leadership—one that inspires through presence and conviction—creates movements, not just moments. When individuals live out Big Faith, they light a fire in others. They invite people into a new way of being: one rooted in love, clarity, and courage. And as more people catch that spark, the momentum grows. Not by force, but by resonance. Not through coercion, but through inspiration. This is how movements are born—not just through big declarations, but through the consistent, courageous living of those who dare to believe differently.

Creating Positive Change with "Big Faith Little Religion"

Combining Big Faith and Little Religion: A Powerful Catalyst for Change

When Big Faith and Little Religion come together, something transformative happens. Big Faith carries the weight of conviction, vision, and purpose—while Little Religion makes room for flexibility, curiosity, and innovation. The synergy between the two unlocks not only personal freedom but the creative energy needed to imagine and build a better world. Rather than clinging to rigid doctrines or binary thinking, this integrated approach allows individuals to see nuance. They are no longer trapped by outdated religious forms, nor are they detached from deep spiritual conviction. It's a dynamic posture that invites both reverence and questioning, tradition and renewal. As Karen Armstrong reminds us, *"True spirituality is always context-driven. It evolves as we grow in empathy, awareness, and love."* (Armstrong, 2009) [7] Her words reflect the spirit of Little Religion—faith that breathes, moves, and responds to the world's needs without losing its soul. This combined force becomes especially powerful in addressing real-world challenges. Big Faith gives individuals the courage to take action, while

Little Religion offers the humility to adapt, listen, and learn. It creates a faith that doesn't just talk about change—but becomes change.

As social marketing pioneer Nancy Lee puts it, *"Lasting change is driven by values, sustained by empathy, and scaled through collaboration."* (Lee, 2001) [8] These are the very qualities that emerge when Big Faith and Little Religion join forces. In a world hungry for both conviction and compassion, combining these two approaches becomes more than a belief system—it becomes a catalyst for renewal. A spark for justice. A framework for creating the kind of change that doesn't burn out but burns brighter with every act of love, truth, and courage.

Freedom from Dogma: Embracing a More Open and Inclusive Approach

The integration of Big Faith and Little Religion offers a liberating path— one that frees individuals from the weight of rigid dogma and traditional religious constraint. It invites a more open and inclusive spiritual posture, where questions are welcomed, doubts are explored, and faith becomes a lived experience rather than a fixed formula. As theologian Hans Küng put it, *"No one can prove God, but everyone can experience God."* (Küng, 1974) [9] This kind of faith is not built on conformity to prescribed doctrine, but on a deep, personal connection to the sacred. It leaves room for nuance, context, and discovery— encouraging individuals to seek a faith that resonates with their soul, not just their surroundings.

By moving beyond rule-bound religion, people can begin to cultivate a more authentic spiritual life—one shaped by love, humility, and curiosity rather than obligation or fear. This is the freedom that lies at the heart of Big Faith Little Religion: the freedom to think, to wrestle, and to walk with God in a way that is honest and alive.

Practical Applications: Real-World Examples of Big Faith Little Religion in Action

Real-world examples offer compelling evidence of how Big Faith and Little Religion can catalyse meaningful change. One such example is the Civil Rights Movement in the United States, led by figures like Martin Luther King Jr. His unwavering commitment to nonviolent resistance and his faith in the inherent worth and dignity of every individual exemplified the transformative power of this integrated approach (Branch, 1988) [10]. His leadership did not rely on rigid religious structures but on a faith deeply rooted in love, justice, and moral courage—principles that resonated far beyond the church walls and reshaped the course of American history.

In South Africa, the formation of the African National Congress (ANC) in a church in Bloemfontein, Free State Province, also reflects the powerful intersection of faith and justice. Religious leaders played a pivotal role in establishing the ANC, drawing on their spiritual convictions to confront the injustice of apartheid. Their efforts were fuelled not by institutional religion alone, but by a deep, personal faith in equality, compassion, and human dignity. The ANC's ongoing commitment to building a just and equitable society was born from this blend of conviction and courage.

These examples demonstrate how Big Faith—anchored in purpose— and Little Religion—rooted in authenticity—can inspire movements that change the world. They remind us that when faith is expressed in action, unburdened by dogma, it has the power to heal, to unite, and to transform both individuals and nations.

CHAPTER 9

LIVING OUT BIG FAITH LITTLE RELIGION

PRACTICING BIG FAITH LITTLE RELIGION IN EVERYDAY LIFE

Integrating Big Faith Little Religion into Your Daily Routine: Starting Strong

Living out Big Faith Little Religion begins not in grand gestures, but in the quiet consistency of daily practice. How you begin your day can shape the way you experience it. Starting with intention, even in small ways, can set the tone for a grounded, purposeful life.

This might look like a few moments of silence before the world rushes in—a pause to breathe deeply, pray, meditate, or write in a journal. Gratitude, in particular, can be a powerful anchor. As psychologist Robert Emmons explains, *"Gratitude is a powerful tool for spiritual growth and well-being"* (Emmons, 2003) [1]. When practised regularly, it shifts the focus from what's lacking to what's present. It roots the heart in appreciation and opens the mind to possibility.

You don't need to overhaul your life to make space for Big Faith. Even five minutes of stillness in the morning can bring clarity. A short reflection on your values, a question posed in prayer, or a line scribbled in a notebook can centre you. These small habits, repeated daily, create space for faith to grow and deepen—not out of obligation, but out of desire. They remind you of what truly matters, giving strength to face whatever the day brings with calm, courage, and clarity.

Mindfulness and Presence: Living in the Moment

Practising Big Faith Little Religion calls us to be grounded—not in theories, but in the here and now. Being fully present allows us to let go of regrets from the past and anxiety about the future. It brings us back to what is real and unfolding before us.

Mindfulness expert Jon Kabat-Zinn describes it this way: *"**Mindfulness is the practice of paying attention to the present moment with openness, curiosity, and a willingness to be with what is"*** (Kabat-Zinn, 2003) [2]. This kind of presence isn't about escaping reality—it's about meeting it with eyes wide open and a heart that is awake.

You don't need a meditation cushion or a quiet retreat to practise mindfulness. It can happen while sipping tea, walking to your car, or washing dishes. Simply slowing down and noticing your breath, your surroundings, or your emotions in real time is enough. When we do this, even the most ordinary moments become sacred.

Mindfulness nurtures spiritual clarity. It creates space for inner stillness, even when life is loud. And from that stillness, faith grows—quietly, steadily, and deeply. In living this way, we come to see that Big Faith isn't something distant or grand. It's found in the small pauses, in the presence of now, and in the willingness to be fully alive to it.

Incorporating Faith into Daily Activities: Finding Purpose and Meaning

Big Faith Little Religion isn't confined to sacred spaces or quiet moments. It can shape the way you work, love, rest, and contribute—bringing purpose to the ordinary. Whether in your job, your relationships, or your hobbies, faith can become a living, breathing part of your daily rhythm. Psychologist Amy Wrzesniewski explains that, *"When people view their work as a calling, they are more likely to experience a sense of purpose and meaning"* (Wrzesniewski, 2003) [3]. This shift in perspective—from task to calling—can transform the way we move through the world.

When we approach our work with intention, our conversations with love, and our actions with integrity, even the most routine activities take on new significance. Doing the laundry becomes an act of care. Responding kindly becomes a moment of grace. A hard day at work becomes an opportunity to practise patience, presence, and purpose. Living out Big Faith means being attentive to how your choices ripple outward. It may look like volunteering your time, mentoring someone younger, or simply showing up with compassion in your local community. These everyday acts become sacred when rooted in love. This is the heart of spiritual practice—not only believing something, but embodying it. And in doing so, you create a life marked not just by faith, but by impact. One moment, one choice, one act of goodness at a time.

Overcoming Obstacles with Big Faith Little Religion: Finding Strength in the Face of Adversity

Big Faith Little Religion isn't only about moments of triumph—it's about how we walk through difficulty. When life gets hard, when answers are few and the road ahead is unclear, faith becomes our anchor. It's in these very moments that trust in something greater, paired with inner resilience, carries us forward. As author Brené Brown puts it, *"You can choose courage or you can choose comfort. You cannot have both."* (Brown, 2010) [4] This insight reminds us that facing adversity often calls for courage—the kind that doesn't wait for the storm to pass, but walks through it with heart and honesty. Faith doesn't remove our struggles, but it reframes them. Instead of seeing obstacles as reasons to give up, we begin to see them as invitations to grow. Through prayer, community and grounded spiritual practices, we find strength that doesn't come from certainty but from hope. Obstacles become turning points. Fear becomes fuel. And even in the darkest moments, Big Faith Little Religion gives us permission to believe: that we are not alone and that we have what it takes to rise.

Facing Fear and Doubt: The Power of Trust

Fear and doubt have a way of paralysing us. They cloud our judgement, steal our peace and convince us that we are not enough. But Big Faith invites us to see through a different lens—a lens of trust. Not blind trust, but courageous trust. The kind that says, *"I don't know how this will turn out, but I believe I will not be alone in it."* Trusting in a higher power doesn't mean pretending everything is fine. It means choosing to believe that there is meaning, even in the mess. That setbacks don't have the final word. That what we're walking through can shape us, not just shake us. Big Faith replaces paralysis with movement. It replaces fear with focus, and doubt with a deeper dependence on truth that holds steady even when life doesn't.

Embracing Adversity: The Art of Resilience

Adversity can either break us or build us—it all depends on how we meet it. In the spirit of Big Faith Little Religion, hardship isn't a punishment, it's an invitation. An invitation to grow, to stretch, to deepen. Psychologist Martin Seligman describes this perspective as *"learned optimism"*—the ability to view challenges as stepping stones, not stumbling blocks (Seligman, 2011) [5]. When we shift our posture from resistance to openness, adversity becomes a teacher rather than a threat. This kind of resilience doesn't come from pretending everything is okay. It comes from faith rooted in something real. It's the quiet confidence that says, *"Even here, even now—I am being shaped."* And in that shaping, we become more grounded, more compassionate, more ourselves.

Finding Strength in Vulnerability: The Power of Humility

Big Faith Little Religion isn't about having all the answers—it's about having the courage to admit when you don't. At the heart of this faith is a quiet strength that comes from embracing vulnerability, not hiding from it. Vulnerability is not weakness. It's the doorway to depth, to intimacy, and to real spiritual growth. Researcher Brené Brown reminds us, *"Vulnerability is the birthplace of love, acceptance, and compassion.*" (Brown, 2012) [6]. In other words, when we let go of our armour and show up as we truly are—imperfect, uncertain, human—we make room for grace to meet us there.

Humility begins when we realise we are not in control, and we don't have to be. We learn to depend not on our own strength alone, but on something greater. And in that surrender, something powerful happens: our hearts soften, our faith deepens, and we start to see others with new eyes.

Living with vulnerability allows us to face life not as performers, but as participants—honest, present, and open. And that openness becomes the ground on which true transformation takes place.

Staying Motivated on Your Big Faith Little Religion Journey: Strategies for Success

Celebrating Small Wins: The Power of Progress

Acknowledging and celebrating small victories is essential for staying motivated on your Big Faith journey. These moments of progress, no matter how modest, build confidence and create momentum for what lies ahead. As leadership consultant John Maxwell wisely notes, *"Small disciplines repeated with consistency every day lead to great achievements gained slowly over time."* (Maxwell, 2006) [7]. His insight reminds us that real transformation rarely happens all at once—it unfolds step by step, through faithful practice. Celebrating small wins can be as simple as pausing to reflect on what's going well, journaling moments of growth, or sharing a personal breakthrough with someone close. These acts of recognition help strengthen belief, reinforce meaningful habits, and inject joy into the journey. Over time, these small celebrations become anchors of encouragement that keep you moving forward with purpose and clarity.

Finding Support and Accountability: The Power of Community

Surrounding yourself with supportive people who share your values and passions is crucial for staying motivated on your Big Faith Little Religion journey. By finding support and accountability, individuals can cultivate a sense of community and belonging.—As community builder Jean Vanier once said, *"One of the marvelous things about community is that it enables us to welcome and help people in a way we couldn't as individuals."* (Vanier, 1998) [8] His words remind us that spiritual strength often grows best in the soil of shared purpose and compassionate connection. Finding support and accountability can involve joining a community group or organisation that reflects your values, attending events that inspire growth, or simply spending time with people who encourage and uplift you. A strong, value-aligned community offers not just companionship, but also clarity, motivation, and the steady reminder that you're not alone. By incorporating these strategies into your daily life, you can stay motivated, inspired, and committed to your Big Faith Little Religion journey. Remember to celebrate your small wins, surround yourself with supportive people, and stay focused on your goals. With persistence, determination, and faith, you can overcome any obstacle and achieve greatness.

Practicing Self-Care and Self-Compassion: Essential for a Thriving Big Faith Little Religion Journey

Prioritising self-care and self-compassion is essential for staying inspired and resilient on your Big Faith Little Religion journey. When we give ourselves the space to rest, reset, and reflect, we not only preserve our energy—we deepen our capacity for faith. As researcher Kristin Neff explains, *"Self-compassion is the practice of treating oneself with kindness, understanding, and acceptance."* (Neff, 2011) [9]. It means speaking to yourself the way you would to someone you love. Self-care is not indulgence—it's survival. Without it, we run dry. Whether it's exercise, prayer, meditation, journaling, time in nature, or simply soaking in a warm bath, these everyday acts of care restore balance and calm. They help us face life's demands from a place of wholeness instead of depletion. Living with self-compassion invites us to embrace our limits. Rather than striving for perfection, we begin to accept ourselves with grace. In doing so, we shed layers of harsh self-judgement and cultivate a gentler, more truthful relationship with ourselves. That kindness clears the way for growth. Incorporating moments of care and compassion into your daily rhythm will transform the way you live, lead, and love. You'll find greater clarity, steadier motivation, and deeper joy. And as your inner life flourishes, so will your ability to pour into others.

Remember—taking care of yourself is not selfish. It's how you keep showing up, with strength, softness, and spirit. It's how you live out Big Faith with integrity and heart.

Embracing Challenges as Opportunities for Growth: A Key Aspect of Big Faith Little Religion

Reframing Challenges: A Positive Perspective

In the Big Faith Little Religion journey, challenges are not just setbacks—they're invitations to grow. When we choose to view difficulty through a lens of possibility, we open ourselves to transformation. This mindset shift, often called *reframing*, allows us to respond with resilience instead of retreat. As resilience expert Diane Coutu writes, ***"Resilient people possess three characteristics: a staunch acceptance of reality; a deep belief that life is meaningful; and an uncanny ability to improvise."*** (Coutu, 2002) [10] This perspective doesn't ignore pain or hardship—it simply refuses to be defined by it. Instead, it asks: *What is this moment teaching me? How might I grow from here?*

Reframing takes practice. It means learning to let go of fear-based narratives and embracing the idea that challenges hold hidden gifts. Practices like mindfulness, reflection, or journaling can help us shift our thinking. Over time, these tools build a mental and spiritual strength that enables us to face life with more grace and courage. Every challenge carries within it a seed of transformation. When we water that seed with hope and faith, it begins to bloom—not in spite of hardship, but because of it.

Finding the Lesson: Seeking Wisdom and Insight

Living out Big Faith Little Religion means being willing to learn from every experience—especially the hard ones. When life doesn't go as planned, the question isn't only *"Why did this happen?"* but *"What is this teaching me?"* As theologian Henri Nouwen once said, ***"Our*** *wounds are often the openings into the best and most beautiful part of us."* (Nouwen, 1994) [11] This reminds us that growth often begins in places of discomfort or disappointment. Finding the lesson calls for honesty, self-reflection, and a desire to grow. It asks us to sit with the experience, examine our own thoughts and reactions, and ask what wisdom we can carry forward. This process doesn't erase pain, but it redeems it—transforming it into something meaningful.

Cultivating Resilience: Bouncing Back from Setbacks

Resilience is not about avoiding challenges—it's about meeting them head-on and rising again with greater strength. In the Big Faith Little Religion journey, setbacks are not signs of failure but stepping stones toward growth. As psychologist Angela Duckworth writes, *"Grit is passion and perseverance for long-term goals."* (Duckworth, 2016) [12] Her research shows that success often depends not on talent or resources, but on our ability to keep going when the path gets tough. Resilience grows when we allow ourselves to be stretched, to learn from failure, and to trust that we're being shaped for something greater. It requires faith, courage, and the choice to keep moving forward.

Practicing Gratitude: Focusing on the Positive

Gratitude is a daily practice that keeps us grounded in hope. In a world that often focuses on what's lacking, gratitude shifts our perspective toward abundance, even in difficult seasons. As author Melody Beattie reminds us, *"Gratitude unlocks the fullness of life. It turns what we have into enough, and more."* (Beattie, 1990) [13] This quote captures the spirit of Big Faith Little Religion—finding joy not just in mountaintop moments, but also in the ordinary. Practicing gratitude can be simple: writing a few thankful thoughts each night, pausing to appreciate a kind gesture, or naming something beautiful you noticed today. Over time, this practice softens our hearts, lifts our spirits, and reminds us that even on hard days, we are not alone.

Embracing Forgiveness: Letting Go of Grudges

Forgiveness is a central part of living out Big Faith Little Religion. It is not about denying the hurt, but about releasing its hold on you. By letting go of grudges, we open the door to peace, healing, and restoration (Enright, 2001) [14]. As psychologist Robert Enright explains, *"Forgiveness is a process of change, where an individual moves from a state of resentment to a state of acceptance."* (Enright, 2001) [14] It's a journey that transforms pain into freedom. Embracing forgiveness takes courage. It means choosing to release someone, not because they deserve it, but because you do. It's about acknowledging the pain but refusing to let it define your story. Forgiveness doesn't condone the wrongdoing; it simply says, *"I choose peace over bitterness."* In doing so, we cultivate compassion, empathy, and a deep sense of inner freedom that strengthens our faith and opens our hearts.

Living Out Big Faith Little Religion: Integrating Faith into Everyday Life

To truly live out Big Faith Little Religion means weaving your values and beliefs into the fabric of daily life. It's not a once-off commitment but a daily choice to align your actions with your inner convictions. Whether through small acts of kindness, quiet moments of prayer, or courageous decisions that reflect your values, this kind of faith shows up in how you live, love, and lead.-As author Anne Lamott writes, *"Hope begins in the dark, the stubborn hope that if you just show up and try to do the right thing, the dawn will come."* (Lamott, 2006) [15] Her words reflect the everyday nature of Big Faith—it's not about perfection, but about showing up with purpose and trust, even when the path ahead is unclear.

Living out this faith means staying anchored in what truly matters, especially when the world is loud, uncertain, or confusing. It's about letting your beliefs guide your choices, not just in grand gestures but in the quiet, consistent rhythms of life. With every mindful step, every act of forgiveness, and every decision made in love, you embody a faith that is alive, grounded, and transformational.

Practicing Mindfulness: Cultivating Awareness and Presence

Mindfulness is a vital part of living out Big Faith Little Religion. It calls us to be fully present—to pay attention to life as it unfolds, rather than being pulled into worry about the future or regret over the past. By cultivating presence, individuals can experience greater clarity, calm, and inner peace, enabling them to navigate life's challenges with faith and composure.

Mindfulness can be practised through quiet meditation, deep breathing, or simply tuning into your surroundings and sensations. Whether you're washing dishes or walking in nature, each moment becomes an opportunity to become more grounded. As this awareness deepens, so does the ability to respond to life with greater wisdom and grace.

Overcoming Obstacles: Building Strength Through Resilience

Challenges are inevitable—but they need not derail your faith journey. Big Faith Little Religion teaches us to face adversity with perseverance. Resilience isn't about avoiding hardship; it's about rising in its midst. It's learning from what's come before and trusting that you can endure what lies ahead.

True resilience also includes knowing when to lean on others. Whether it's prayer, counselling, or the quiet presence of a trusted friend, seeking support can breathe strength into weary hearts. With help and hope, obstacles lose their power to define you.

Staying Motivated: Cultivating Hope and Inspiration

Staying motivated on the Big Faith journey means keeping your heart stirred with hope—even when progress feels slow. Hope acts as fuel, keeping faith alive when the path is unclear or steep. Surrounding yourself with supportive, life-giving people and engaging in joyful, meaningful experiences can reawaken your passion and sense of direction.

Sometimes, motivation is renewed simply by remembering your "why"—the deeper purpose behind your daily choices. Reflecting on your values and seeking guidance through prayer or journaling can help realign your heart and restore your determination to keep going.

Embracing Challenges: Choosing Courage Over Comfort

Big Faith doesn't shrink in the face of uncertainty—it leans in. To embrace challenges is to trust that growth is often disguised as discomfort. Rather than running from difficulty, Big Faith chooses to meet it with courage and an open heart.

This means cultivating a mindset that sees obstacles not as threats, but as invitations to deepen faith and discover hidden strength. It's about taking brave steps—even when you don't have all the answers—and trusting that you're not walking alone.

Cultivating Resilience: Staying the Course with Grit and Grace

To live out Big Faith Little Religion is to keep going when it would be easier to give up. Resilience is what carries you through the storms. It's the grit that keeps your feet moving forward, and the grace that softens your heart in the process.

Building resilience means developing emotional tools for tough seasons, learning from your journey, and welcoming support when needed. Whether through prayer, community, or honest self-reflection, resilience grows each time you choose to stand, stay, and believe.

CHAPTER 10

EMBRACING THE JOURNEY

CONCLUSION

Big Faith Little Religion is not a destination. It's a journey—one of becoming, unfolding, expanding. A journey marked not by perfection, but by intention. A path that welcomes your questions, honours your humanity, and invites your transformation.

Embracing Imperfection: The First Step Towards Growth

Growth begins where perfection ends. You don't need to have it all together to start. In fact, it's your openness that makes you ready. As author Elizabeth Gilbert reflects, *"Embrace the glorious mess that you are."* (Gilbert, 2009) [1] Accepting your limitations is not weakness—it's the doorway to strength. The courage to show up, try again, and let your vulnerability lead is where Big Faith begins.

The Power of Small Beginnings: Creating a Ripple Effect

Tiny actions, taken consistently, can spark transformation. The momentum builds not from grand gestures, but from faithful persistence. As author James Clear puts it, **"Every action you take is a vote for the type of person you wish to become."** (Clear, 2018) [2] Those small, ordinary steps? They're how Big Faith makes its way into real life. One choice at a time. One yes at a time.

Overcoming Fear and Doubt: Taking Action Despite Fear

Fear will whisper, "You're not ready." Doubt will insist, "You'll fail." But Big Faith speaks louder. It urges you to move anyway. As Susan Jeffers reminds us, *"Feel the fear and do it anyway."* (Jeffers, 1987) [3] Action isn't the absence of fear—it's movement in spite of it. You don't wait for certainty; you take a step. And then another. That's how confidence grows.

Taking the First Step with Little Faith: Building Momentum

You don't need Big Faith to begin. You just need a little—a mustard seed's worth. Start with what you have. Trust that momentum will meet you on the way. As author Stephen Covey encourages, *"Begin with the end in mind."* (Covey, 1989) [4]

Clarify your intention. Commit to one step. And let the journey build from there.

Unlocking Your Full Potential: Big Faith Little Religion

Big Faith Little Religion invites you to live with depth and authenticity. It's not about perfect belief—it's about full-hearted living. As spiritual teacher Marianne Williamson says, *"We are all meant to shine, as children do."* (Williamson, 1992) [5] When you live with Big Faith Little

Religion, you open yourself to purpose, to wonder, and to the sacred rhythm of becoming who you were always meant to be.

A Call to Action: Join the Revolution

This isn't a private path. It's a shared one. Find your people—your tribe of seekers, thinkers, lovers of grace and justice. As Seth Godin puts it, *"The tribe is the new factory."* (Godin, 2008) [6]

Your faith expands when it's lived in community. Share the journey. Learn together. Spark change together.

Sustaining Big Faith for the Long Haul

This work is lifelong. It's about grit, not hype. Faithfulness, not flash. As psychologist Angela Duckworth affirms, *"Grit is passion and perseverance for long-term goals."* (Duckworth, 2016) [7] Stay anchored. Celebrate often. Rest well. Return to your centre. Big Faith isn't about endless striving—it's about rooted living.

The Power of Community: Surrounding Yourself with Positive Influences

Your environment shapes your endurance. Choose your circle wisely. Surround yourself with those who lift, stretch, and inspire you. As motivational speaker Jim Rohn famously said, *"You are the average of the five people you spend the most time with."* (Rohn, 2004) [8] Faith grows in good soil. Tend your community, and your roots will go deep.

Finding Accountability Partners: Staying Motivated and Inspired

Finding accountability partners is essential for sustaining Big Faith Little Religion. This involves surrounding yourself with individuals who share your values and goals—people who can walk alongside you, offering encouragement, feedback, and perspective. As psychologist Daniel Goleman notes, *"The most effective leaders are those who are able to build strong relationships with others."* (Goleman, 1995) [9] True accountability thrives in relationships built on trust, empathy, and mutual respect.

It also requires a shared commitment to growth and excellence. As leadership expert Jim Collins writes, *"Those who build great companies understand that the ultimate throttle on growth is not markets or technology or competition or products. It is one thing above all others: the ability to get and keep the right people."* (Collins, 2001) [10] The same is true for faith journeys. The people you journey with—your community, your accountability partners—will either fuel or drain your momentum.

By choosing the right partners, you don't just stay motivated—you grow. You become sharper, more honest, and more inspired to continue walking out your Big Faith Little Religion journey with clarity, consistency, and courage.

Celebrating Small Wins: Staying Motivated and Focused

Celebrating small wins is crucial for sustaining Big Faith Little Religion. This involves acknowledging and celebrating your achievements, no matter how small they may seem. As author Shawn Achor explains, *"Happiness is not the belief that we don't need to change; it is the realisation that we can."* (Achor, 2010) [11] Recognising progress, even in small steps, fuels a sense of hope and reinforces the belief that transformation is possible. By celebrating your small wins—writing them down, sharing them with someone you trust, or simply pausing to reflect—you create moments of momentum. These small victories become stepping stones, keeping you motivated, focused, and inspired on your Big Faith Little Religion journey.

Cultivating Grit and Resilience: Overcoming Obstacles and Achieving Greatness

Cultivating grit and resilience is essential for sustaining Big Faith. This involves developing a growth mindset, being open to learning and growth, and being willing to take calculated risks. As author Elizabeth Gilbert writes, *"Resilience is our shared genetic inheritance. It's in our DNA. You may not have seen it in yourself yet, but I guarantee you— your resilience is there."* (Gilbert, 2015) [12] Resilience doesn't mean avoiding failure; it means rising again with courage and curiosity. By choosing to persevere, to adapt, and to keep going even when the road is hard, you grow stronger. You discover grit not as something extraordinary, but as a quiet, steady decision to show up—again and again—with faith.

Sustaining Big Faith Little Religion requires a commitment to perseverance, celebration, and community. By surrounding yourself with positive influences, finding accountability partners, celebrating small wins, and cultivating grit and resilience, you can overcome obstacles, stay motivated, and achieve greatness. Remember, Big Faith is a journey, not a destination. Stay committed, stay focused, and you will walk in the fullness of what was always possible.

Overcoming Obstacles with Big Faith Little Religion

Anticipating challenges and developing strategies for overcoming them is crucial for sustaining Big Faith Little Religion. As psychologist Albert Bandura notes, *"People who have a strong sense of self-efficacy are more likely to take on challenges and persist in the face of obstacles."* (Bandura, 1997) [13] By anticipating challenges, individuals can prepare themselves for what lies ahead and develop effective coping strategies.

Persevering through adversity is essential for living out Big Faith. As theologian Paul Tillich notes, *"Faith is the courage to be in spite of the fact that we are finite and vulnerable."* (Tillich, 1957) [14] Big Faith Little Religion provides the resilience and determination needed to overcome obstacles and remain grounded in one's values and vision. As individuals persist through hardship, their faith deepens, and their sense of purpose becomes more refined.

Celebrating Milestones and Progress Along the Way

Acknowledging small wins is essential for sustaining motivation and momentum on the Big Faith Little Religion journey. Small victories are not just incidental—they are signs that transformation is already taking place. By celebrating them, individuals build confidence and reinforce their commitment to a life of purpose.

Reflecting on progress is also vital for identifying areas of growth and redirecting efforts where needed. As psychologist Daniel Goleman notes, *"Self-awareness is the ability to monitor our thoughts, feelings, and actions, and to use this awareness to guide our behaviour."* (Goleman, 1995) [16] Through intentional reflection, individuals gain greater insight into their patterns and are better equipped to adjust their course when necessary, all while staying rooted in their Big Faith journey.

PART II

LITTLE FAITH GREAT MIRACLES

LITTLE FAITH, GREAT MIRACLES: YOUR LITTLE FAITH IS BIG ENOUGH

"Faith is a prerequisite for bringing unseen things into reality." — **Godwin Booysen**

Faith doesn't have to be loud or certain to be real. Sometimes, it shows up as a whisper in the dark. A fragile hope. A hesitant prayer. And yet, even in its smallest form, faith carries the potential to shift the atmosphere around us.

As someone who has walked through valleys of doubt and uncertainty, I understand what it feels like to be disconnected from the world around you. It's easy to lose sight of the beauty and wonder of life when we're overwhelmed by our circumstances. But what if I told you that even in the darkest of times, there is always hope?

The Bible reminds us that *"the people who know their God shall be strong, and carry out great exploits"* (Daniel 11:32b). This verse has been a continual source of inspiration for me, and I believe it can be for you as well.

In the chapters ahead, we will explore biblical examples of faith and miracles, alongside inspiring stories drawn from other philosophies, traditions, and cultures. My goal is not to convince you to adopt a particular theological viewpoint. Rather, I hope to encourage you to re-examine your own faith and relationship with the divine. Whether you are a lifelong believer or simply someone searching for deeper meaning, I invite you to walk with me through this journey of discovery. Together, we'll reflect on the lives of ordinary people who accomplished extraordinary things through their faith. We'll look at the principles and practices that helped them persevere through impossible odds and walk in miraculous outcomes.

As we begin, I want to remind you that it's perfectly okay to start small. You don't need to have *great* faith to see *great* miracles. Jesus said that even faith as small as a mustard seed can move mountains (Matthew 17:20; Mark 11:23).

So, if you are feeling discouraged, disconnected, or doubtful—hold on. There is still hope. Let's discover together how little faith can lead to great miracles, and how trusting in something greater than ourselves can reshape everything.

When people speak of faith, they often mean confidence, trust, or reliance—whether in something, someone, or even in an unseen promise.

And if I may be honest, I feel I may not have done full justice to the subject of faith in the first two parts of the book on *Big Faith Little*

Religion. Faith is complex and deeply personal, and its object can vary widely. Here are just a few examples...

Expressions of Faith: Religious, Secular, and Philosophical

Religious Faith

Religious faith remains one of the most profound and personal aspects of human experience. For many, it begins with belief in God or a higher power who guides, protects, and provides meaning to life. This trust forms the foundation of their spiritual journey, offering comfort and strength through all seasons.

Faith is often not only placed in a divine being, but also in sacred teachings, scriptures, and doctrines. The Bible defines faith as *"the substance of things hoped for, the evidence of things not seen"* (Hebrews 11:1–3, KJV). It is a powerful picture: faith becomes the unseen bridge between what we hope for and what we eventually see come to pass. It is, in many ways, the prerequisite for transforming the invisible into reality.

For some, faith is nurtured through spiritual practices—prayer, meditation, fasting, worship, or disciplines like yoga. These practices are not rituals for the sake of tradition but pathways to inner peace, divine connection, and daily renewal. They help cultivate a deeper sense of spiritual grounding and lead to a more meaningful and purpose-filled life.

Secular Faith

Faith is not limited to the spiritual realm. Secular faith also plays a vital role in how we navigate the world. This type of faith takes shape as trust—trust in systems, in people, in progress, and in ourselves.

For many, that trust is anchored in science and reason. They place faith in the scientific method, in empirical evidence, and in the pursuit of truth through logic and observation. It is a belief that the world operates according to knowable laws, and that through exploration and understanding, we can uncover the mysteries of life and improve the human condition. Secular faith is also deeply social. People put their faith in the goodness of humanity, in the power of community, and in the possibility of justice. It is the kind of faith that drives movements for equality, inspires social progress, and fuels the belief that collective action can make a meaningful difference in the world.

Perhaps most personally, secular faith shows up as belief in oneself. It's the quiet confidence that says, *I can do this*. Faith in our own resilience, our capacity to learn and grow, and our ability to rise after falling—this inner trust empowers people to step beyond fear, take risks, and pursue goals with courage. It's the faith that allows us to keep showing up, even when the way forward is unclear.

Philosophical Faith

Philosophical faith takes a more reflective shape. It's the faith we place in ideas—often abstract, yet deeply influential.

One such idea is *free will*. Many believe in the power of human choice: that individuals are not merely shaped by circumstance, but that they have agency to shape their own lives. This belief underpins moral responsibility and the conviction that our decisions matter. Faith in free

157

will affirms that we are not powerless, even when life feels unpredictable or overwhelming.

Metaphysical Faith

Metaphysics, a branch of philosophy concerned with the nature of reality, invites us to reflect on the unseen foundations of existence. It asks the deeper questions—about being and becoming, mind and matter, potential and purpose. While metaphysics stands as its own field of inquiry, it often intertwines with philosophical faith. Together, they shape how we understand the world and our place within it. Philosophical faith, in this context, is not just a belief in ideas, but a trust in the frameworks through which we interpret reality. Whether we are pondering the existence of the soul, the relationship between consciousness and the body, or the fabric of time and causality, metaphysical thought provides a foundation upon which faith in the unseen or unknown can rest.

Free Will: A Cornerstone of Moral Agency

Among the most enduring and debated metaphysical ideas is the concept of *free will*. At its heart, free will refers to our capacity to choose—to make decisions that are not solely dictated by genetics, environment, or the chain of past events. It suggests that we are not passive products of fate, but active participants in shaping our lives.

This idea carries weighty implications, especially when it comes to moral responsibility. Philosopher P.F. Strawson, writing in 1962, argued that free will is essential if we are to hold individuals morally accountable. Without the freedom to choose, the grounds for praise or blame begin to unravel. But if we accept that people do have agency—that they are able to deliberate, decide, and act from within their own will—then we must also recognise their moral responsibility. Faith in free will allows us to see people not just as shaped by circumstance, but as capable of growth, change, and redemption. It affirms personal agency, even amid adversity, and it demands that we treat others as moral beings capable of both error and excellence.

Of course, the debate around free will remains ongoing. Philosophy, psychology, and neuroscience all contribute perspectives—some challenging, others affirming the notion that we are truly free in our decision-making. Yet despite the differing views, what remains clear is this: *the belief in free will shapes how we see ourselves and others*. It undergirds our concepts of justice, ethics, and human dignity. And it invites us to walk through life not as victims of fate, but as those entrusted with the sacred task of choice.

Faith as a Choice

Faith, at its heart, is not just something we receive—it is something we choose. This choice becomes especially powerful when we find ourselves searching for meaning, direction, or hope. The philosophical tradition of **existentialism** speaks directly to this human longing. It recognises our deep desire to make sense of life, to rise above the noise and confusion, and to live with intention. In that search, faith becomes not just a comfort, but a compass.

Choosing faith is choosing meaning. It gives us a reason to keep going when life doesn't make sense. It connects us to something greater than ourselves—something unseen yet deeply felt. That connection brings with it a sense of belonging and purpose. When we choose to believe, even when it would be easier not to, we are saying, "There is more to this life than what I see." Faith doesn't remove life's hardships, but it does transform how we move through them. It lifts us out of despair. It roots us when the ground beneath us feels uncertain. It says, *you are not alone*. In this way, faith becomes a quiet rebellion against fear, isolation, and cynicism. It helps us stand firm—not because everything is certain, but because something greater is holding us.

This sense of belonging—of being seen, known, and held—is one of the most healing gifts of faith. When we see ourselves as part of a divine story or spiritual community, our pain no longer isolates us. Instead, it becomes part of a shared human experience. Faith reminds us that we matter, and that even our small, imperfect steps are part of something sacred.

But what of those who question whether faith is truly a choice? Some traditions suggest that faith is divinely given, while others see it as something we develop through practice, curiosity, and lived experience. This question matters. Because if faith is predetermined, how do we hold people responsible for belief or unbelief? What does that mean for sin, or for the possibility of grace? These are not just theological questions—they are human ones.

This tension draws us into deeper reflection. **Metaphysics**, the philosophical study of reality, offers different frameworks for understanding where faith fits in the grand scheme of things. A *materialist* worldview might argue that faith is a by-product of culture, psychology, or neurobiology. In contrast, a *theistic* metaphysics would suggest that faith is a spiritual connection to a divine presence—something real, though not visible.

How we interpret faith depends greatly on which of these lenses we look through. A materialist might see faith as an evolutionary coping mechanism. A theist might see it as the soul's response to God. But both are trying to answer the same question: *What is real?* And that's the invitation of this journey—to explore how faith and reality meet. To ask: Is faith simply a story we tell ourselves to survive? Or is it the thread that connects us to something eternal? Whatever our answer, the act of wrestling with these questions deepens our understanding of what it means to be human.

Faith, then, is not blind acceptance, but courageous inquiry. It is not the absence of doubt, but the willingness to move forward in its presence. Whether found in prayer, reflection, or a quiet moment of surrender, faith remains one of the most profound and personal choices we make. And it's a choice we're invited to make—not just once, but again and again, especially when life grows dark.

Cultural and Social Faith

Faith does not only reside in the spiritual or philosophical realms. It is also expressed through culture, community, and shared social ideals. Many people anchor their beliefs in a collective identity—one shaped by nationality, tradition, justice, and belonging. This form of faith is not always religious, but it is deeply felt, fiercely defended, and profoundly influential in shaping decisions.

National Identity

For some, faith in national identity is a powerful and defining force. It's not merely about citizenship or legal status, but about history, language, memory, and belonging. National identity carries the weight of ancestry, land, and cultural heritage—and when threatened, it can evoke strong, emotional responses. A recent example that stirred public debate is the case involving AfriForum, a South African civil rights organisation representing Afrikaner interests. In response to reported discussions around the United States offering asylum to White Afrikaners, some members of the community, including AfriForum, publicly rejected the idea. For them, leaving South Africa is not just a geographic shift—it is seen as abandoning the legacy of their forefathers.

Ernst Roets, Deputy CEO of AfriForum, articulated this sentiment clearly:

"Our forefathers built this country... We will not abandon it." (Roets, 2022) [1]

This reaction reveals the depth of faith many Afrikaners have in their cultural and national identity. South Africa is not just where they live—it is who they are. Their language, history, and traditions are bound to the soil. To leave would not only be a political or economic decision but a surrender of identity itself.

Faith in national identity, then, becomes a form of spiritual and cultural resistance. It is a commitment to continuity, a refusal to sever ties with the past, and an assertion of presence—even when that presence is contested.

Social Justice

At the same time, the AfriForum case has ignited discussions around another powerful form of faith: the belief in social justice. While some defend their stance in the name of cultural preservation, others critique it as a veiled attempt to retain long-standing privilege in a country still healing from the wounds of apartheid.

For many South Africans, especially Black communities who continue to bear the scars of systemic oppression, the refusal of certain Afrikaners to engage in national transformation feels dissonant. Critics argue that choosing to stay must also include a willingness to confront one's historical complicity and current position within systems of inequality.

In this context, faith in social justice is not merely aspirational—it is foundational. It is rooted in the belief that the future of South Africa depends on acknowledging the past, redressing inequality, and working toward collective healing. It is a faith that drives movements for equity, land reform, education access, and economic redress.

The words of Nelson Mandela still echo through this struggle:

"The greatest glory in living lies not in never falling, but in rising every time we fall." (Mandela, 1993) [2]

This vision of rising is not individual—it is national. And for many, it requires all citizens, including historically advantaged groups, to participate actively in creating a just and inclusive society.

Community and Tradition

Beneath both perspectives—whether national identity or social justice—lies a shared belief in the value of community and tradition. These bonds shape our worldview, giving us language, values, and belonging. For some, that tradition must be preserved at all costs. For others, it must evolve to include those who were once excluded. Faith in community, when grounded in humility and openness, can bridge divides. But when rigid and insular, it can deepen them. The challenge for South Africa—and for many nations—is to find a way to honour tradition without idolising it, and to pursue justice without erasing identity.

In this tension, faith becomes both a compass and a mirror. It asks: *What are we holding onto? And why? Are we preserving life, or preserving power? Are we building together, or standing apart?*

Community and Tradition

The AfriForum asylum debate also highlights the vital role of community and tradition in shaping both individual and collective faith. For many Afrikaaners, their community and cultural heritage serve as deep wells of strength, identity, and continuity.

The thought of leaving South Africa and starting anew in a foreign country is not just daunting due to practical challenges—it also carries an emotional and psychological weight. To depart would mean severing ties with a history, a shared language, and a way of life that has been nurtured for generations.

This deep-rooted faith in community and tradition is echoed in the words of AfriForum's Deputy CEO, Ernst Roets: "We will not abandon our forefathers' legacy... We will not abandon our language, our culture, and our traditions" (Roets, 2022) [3].

The AfriForum asylum debate, therefore, offers a rich case study in the layered and often contested terrain of Cultural and Social Faith. It reveals how national identity, the pursuit of social justice, and a strong commitment to community and tradition converge to shape people's convictions, behaviours, and sense of belonging.

PERSONAL FAITH

Personal faith is a deeply intimate and subjective experience, unique to each individual. It can take many forms and serve as a guiding force in one's life. At its core, personal faith reflects an internal trust—whether in oneself, in the power of relationships, in moral convictions, or in the journey of growth. It shapes how we view the world and respond to life's challenges.

For some, personal faith is intricately tied to the pursuit of self-improvement. These individuals believe in their ability to learn, grow, and become better through education, reflection, or the lessons found in struggle. This inner belief often becomes a powerful motivator—driving people to push beyond their perceived limits and pursue excellence with purpose and resolve.

Others find personal faith in the strength of love and connection. They believe that meaningful relationships—with family, friends, and community—hold the power to heal, uplift, and bring fulfilment. This form of faith recognises the sacredness of human bonds and inspires people to cultivate deeper, more authentic relationships, creating a life anchored in joy and belonging.

Another vital dimension of personal faith is rooted in values and moral conviction. Many individuals trust their inner compass—the set of principles that governs their decisions and actions. This quiet assurance becomes a source of resilience, enabling them to stand firm even in turbulent times. Faith in one's own values provides a sense of consistency, integrity, and clarity amidst a world that often pulls in many directions.

Ultimately, personal faith is not one thing—it is many things. It varies from person to person, influenced by one's history, experiences, and worldview. One individual may find it in daily prayer; another in pursuing justice, or in simply believing that growth is possible.

One of the most profound expressions of personal faith is the belief in one's potential for growth. This is closely related to the idea of self-actualisation, a concept introduced by Abraham Maslow in 1943 [1], which refers to the process of realising one's full potential and becoming the most authentic version of oneself.

When we believe that we can grow, we are more likely to take risks, set goals, and step beyond what feels safe. This belief can become the engine of personal transformation. As Albert Bandura (1997) [1] observed, individuals with strong self-efficacy—a belief in their ability to succeed—are more resilient in the face of difficulty and more persistent in pursuing their goals. Faith in one's ability to change, adapt, and improve forms the foundation for this mindset.

By holding onto personal faith—whether in growth, connection, purpose, or inner wisdom—individuals open themselves up to transformation. This kind of faith doesn't promise perfection, but it makes space for progress. It doesn't deny hardship, but it brings meaning to it.

In essence, personal faith is a quiet, steady force. It enables people to move forward, even when the path is unclear. By nurturing this faith, we unlock potential, live with intention, and build lives rooted in authenticity and hope.

Relationships: Faith in the Power of Connection

Relationships are a profound expression of personal faith. For many people, the love and connection found in meaningful relationships provide a deep well of joy, purpose, and belonging. This kind of faith is grounded in the belief that nurturing those bonds brings strength, comfort, and clarity to life's journey. The importance of strong social ties cannot be underestimated. Research has shown that meaningful connections are not only emotionally enriching but also play a key role in both physical and mental wellbeing (Holt-Lunstad et al., 2015) [3]. When we prioritise genuine connection, we tap into something essential to human flourishing. Having faith in the power of relationships inspires us to be present, intentional, and generous in the way we relate to others. Whether through friendship, family, or community, these connections offer support in times of hardship and celebration in seasons of joy. They become the anchors that hold us steady and the mirrors that reflect our worth.

We are not meant to navigate life alone. Through shared stories, mutual care, and the simple act of being known, we discover strength we may not have found on our own. Faith in the power of connection reminds us that love, at its core, is not a feeling to chase but a commitment to nurture—and when we do, it shapes our lives in powerful, enduring ways.

Personal Values: Faith in Moral Principles

Personal values form the backbone of how many people live out their faith. These values—whether rooted in honesty, compassion, justice, or courage—act as an internal compass. When someone places trust in their moral convictions, they are guided by a deep belief that these principles will hold steady even when everything else feels uncertain. This kind of faith doesn't always look spiritual, but it is deeply personal. It allows individuals to move through life with clarity and purpose. Decisions become less about pleasing others or avoiding discomfort, and more about staying aligned with what matters most. As psychologist Martin Seligman has noted, a strong sense of values is closely linked to greater life satisfaction and psychological wellbeing (Seligman, 2011) [4].

Living according to one's values often requires courage. When pressures arise—whether from society, relationships, or personal fear—values offer a place to stand. That quiet commitment to doing what is right, even when it's not easy, creates integrity. And integrity builds trust, not only with others but within ourselves.

Faith in personal values also provides endurance. When life becomes difficult, returning to our principles gives us a sense of direction. It reminds us who we are and what we stand for. This inner alignment brings peace, even in struggle, and allows us to move forward without losing ourselves in the process.

Living by your values doesn't mean life will always be clear or simple. But it does mean that even in uncertainty, you'll have a foundation to return to—one built not on changing circumstances, but on the steady ground of your own truth.

RELIGIOUS FAITH

Biblical Stories: Learning Faith through Scripture

The Bible is rich with stories that reveal the power of faith. These stories remind us that faith is not just belief—it is trust in God's character, obedience to His voice, and confidence in His promises, even when the outcome is uncertain.

David and Goliath – Faith in God's Strength

(1 Samuel 17)

David's courage in facing Goliath wasn't based on his skill or size but on his faith in God. As a young shepherd, he had no armour, no sword— only a slingshot and trust in the God who had delivered him before.

"The Lord who rescued me from the paw of the lion and the paw of the bear will rescue me from the hand of this Philistine." (1 Samuel 17:37) David's story reminds us that true strength comes from faith, not circumstance.

The Widow of Zarephath – Faith in God's Provision
(1 Kings 17:8–16)

In a time of famine, a poor widow chose to give her last meal to the prophet Elijah, trusting God would provide. Her act of faith ensured that her jar of flour and jug of oil never ran dry.

This story reveals how trust in God, even in moments of lack, unlocks His provision.

The Woman with the Issue of Blood – Faith that Reaches Out
(Matthew 9:20–22; Mark 5:25–34; Luke 8:43–48)

After twelve years of suffering, this woman believed that touching Jesus' cloak would be enough. Her quiet act of faith didn't go unnoticed.

"Take heart, daughter; your faith has healed you." (Matthew 9:22) Faith doesn't always need words. Sometimes, it's the reach of a hand in hope that moves heaven.

Peter Walks on Water – Faith That Wavers but Still Matters
(Matthew 14:22–33)

At Jesus' call, Peter stepped out onto the water. For a moment, his faith held him. But as the wind rose and fear crept in, he began to sink. Even then, Jesus reached out and saved him.

Peter's story reminds us that faith isn't about never doubting—it's about who we turn to when we do.

The Blind Men – Faith that Sees Beyond Sight
(Matthew 9:27–31)

Two blind men followed Jesus, crying out for mercy. When He asked if they believed He could heal them, they said yes.

"According to your faith let it be done to you." (Matthew 9:29) Their eyes were opened. Sometimes the clearest vision is born from faith, not sight.

Hannah – Faith That Perseveres in Prayer
(1 Samuel 1–2)

Hannah's long wait for a child was marked by deep sorrow, yet she never stopped praying. Her faith was rooted in trust that God hears. When her son Samuel was born, she dedicated him to the Lord. Hannah shows us what it looks like to wait in hope, and to trust that prayer is never wasted.

Abraham – Faith in the Promise
(Genesis 15:1–6; Romans 4:18–22)

Despite his old age, Abraham believed God's promise of a son.

"Abram believed the Lord, and He credited it to him as righteousness." (Genesis 15:6)

Abraham teaches us that faith holds on—even when there is nothing visible to hold onto.

Moses and the Red Sea – Faith in God's Power to Deliver
(Exodus 14:13–31)

With the sea before him and Pharaoh's army behind, Moses trusted God and raised his staff. The waters parted, and the Israelites crossed on dry land.

Faith can make a way where there seems to be none.

Joshua and the Walls of Jericho – Faith in God's Strategy
(Joshua 6:1–27)

Joshua followed God's unusual instruction to march around Jericho for seven days. On the seventh day, the walls fell.

Obedience, even when it makes no earthly sense, is an act of faith. God honours it.

Job – Faith in God's Sovereignty Amid Suffering
(Job 1–42)

Job lost everything—his family, his wealth, his health. Yet he said:

"The Lord gave and the Lord has taken away; blessed be the name of the Lord." (Job 1:21)

Though he questioned, grieved, and wrestled, Job never abandoned his faith in God's goodness. His story shows that faith does not mean having all the answers. It means trusting the One who does.

The Centurion – Faith that Recognises True Authority
(Matthew 8:5–13; Luke 7:1–10)

A Roman centurion asked Jesus to heal his servant, saying,

"Just say the word, and my servant will be healed." (Matthew 8:8) Jesus marvelled at his faith, calling it greater than any He had seen in Israel. True faith recognises that God's word carries power, even from a distance.

Living Faith: What These Stories Teach Us
These stories don't just inspire—they instruct. Each one shows us a different facet of faith: courage, trust, obedience, perseverance, humility. Faith is not just a private belief—it moves, speaks, waits, and walks.

Scripture reminds us: "Know therefore that the Lord your God is God; He is the faithful God, keeping His covenant of love to a thousand generations of those who love Him and keep His commandments." (Deuteronomy 7:9)

"Many are the plans in a person's heart, but it is the Lord's purpose that prevails." (Proverbs 19:21)

True faith doesn't demand perfect understanding. It trusts in a perfect God. And it lives in such a way that the world sees not only what we believe—but who we believe in.

APPLYING LITTLE FAITH GREAT MIRACLES TO EVERYDAY LIFE

The idea of "little faith, great miracles" isn't reserved for dramatic moments or extraordinary circumstances. It's a principle we can live by each day. When we learn to trust God in the small, ordinary moments of life, we create space for the extraordinary to unfold.

1. Practising Faith in Daily Life

Living by faith begins with choosing trust over fear in the everyday. It's a posture of the heart—leaning on God's character, even when we can't see the outcome. This kind of faith doesn't wait for certainty. It begins where we are, with what we have.

One of the most powerful ways to build that kind of faith is through consistent, honest conversation with God. Prayer isn't about performance—it's about presence. In quiet moments of prayer and reflection, we learn to surrender our fears and lean into His promises.

Jesus reminds us, *"If you believe, you will receive whatever you ask for in prayer"* (Matthew 21:22). Reading Scripture helps ground that belief. God's Word reveals His nature, His promises, and His faithfulness across generations. As Paul writes, *"Faith comes from hearing the message, and the message is heard through the word about Christ"* (Romans 10:17). Regular time in Scripture shapes our thinking and reminds us of what's true—especially when circumstances tell a different story. Gratitude is another quiet but powerful act of faith. When we thank God—not just for the big breakthroughs, but for breath in our lungs, meals on the table, and glimpses of beauty in the mundane—we train our hearts to see His hand, even in the unseen. As Paul encourages, *"Give thanks in all circumstances, for this is God's will for you in Christ Jesus"* (1 Thessalonians 5:18).

Faith doesn't always feel grand or bold. Sometimes, it's simply showing up, choosing joy, or whispering a prayer when we're unsure. But those small, everyday decisions—those "little faith" moments—can open the door to great miracles. One prayer, one act of trust, one grateful heart at a time.

2. Overcoming Fear and Doubt

Fear and doubt are part of being human. They creep in during times of uncertainty, testing our ability to trust God's goodness and promises. If left unchecked, they can cloud our vision and shrink our faith. But when we face them honestly and bring them before God, they can become a doorway to deeper trust.

The first step is to acknowledge them. Faith doesn't mean pretending we're not afraid—it means we bring our fears to the One who can carry them. Naming our emotions and laying them before God is a powerful act of surrender. As the Psalmist writes, *"My sacrifice, O God, is a broken spirit; a broken and contrite heart you, God, will not despise"* (Psalm 51:17). In moments of vulnerability, God meets us with grace.

Fear and doubt often grow louder through the words we speak to ourselves. Negative thoughts can spiral quickly, feeding feelings of inadequacy and discouragement. But we have the power to interrupt that cycle. When we catch ourselves spiralling, we can speak truth instead. Paul urges us to set our minds on what is life-giving: *"Whatever is true, whatever is noble, whatever is right... think about such things"* (Philippians 4:8). Replacing fearful thoughts with truth helps shift our inner posture from worry to worship.

Another way to quiet fear is to remember. Think back on the times God came through—when prayers were answered, provision arrived just in time, or peace came when it made no sense. These moments aren't just memories—they are anchors. Moses reminded the Israelites, *"The Lord your God is God; he is the faithful God, keeping his covenant of love to a thousand generations"* (Deuteronomy 7:9). When we recall His faithfulness, our confidence is renewed.

Fear and doubt may still knock at the door—but they don't have to stay. As we learn to name them, replace them, and remember God's goodness, we create space for faith to rise again. Even small steps of trust can shift our perspective and prepare the ground for miracles.

3. Embracing Uncertainty and Trusting in God's Plan

Uncertainty is part of life. It often unsettles us, stirring up anxiety as we long for answers and control. Yet in those very moments, when the path ahead is unclear, we're invited into something deeper—a quiet trust in God's plan that brings peace, even when nothing around us makes sense.

One of the biggest hurdles we face is our need to be in control. We try to shape outcomes, predict the future, and make things go according to our plans. But that effort often leads to frustration and fear, because no matter how hard we try, life remains unpredictable. Letting go doesn't mean giving up—it means acknowledging that God is in charge. As Proverbs reminds us, *"Many are the plans in a person's heart, but it is the Lord's purpose that prevails"* (Proverbs 19:21). Instead of striving to control the unknown, we can choose to stay present. Worrying about tomorrow drains today of its peace. Jesus spoke directly to this when He said, *"Do not worry about tomorrow, for tomorrow will worry about itself. Each day has enough trouble of its own"* (Matthew 6:34). When we anchor ourselves in the present, we begin to notice God's hand at work—even in the ordinary, even in the waiting.

At the heart of embracing uncertainty is trust. Even when we don't understand the why or the how, we can lean into the truth that God is good. His plans may not always be clear, but they are always kind. As Paul wrote, *"We know that in all things God works for the good of those who love him, who have been called according to his purpose"* (Romans 8:28). That promise gives us confidence, not just in the outcome, but in the One who holds it.

When we let go of our need to control, stay rooted in the present, and trust in God's goodness, uncertainty becomes less of a threat and more of an invitation. It becomes a space where our faith can grow, where peace can take root, and where God's presence becomes more real than ever.

4. The Power of Community and Support

As we walk out our faith, one truth becomes clear—we were never meant to do it alone. Community isn't just a nice idea; it's essential. Being surrounded by people who encourage, uplift, and walk alongside us can strengthen our faith and help us see God's hand at work in everyday life. A supportive community begins with choosing the right people to journey with. When we spend time with those who speak life into us, challenge us to grow, and share our values, we're more likely to stay rooted in faith. As Proverbs reminds us, *"As iron sharpens iron, so one person sharpens another"* (Proverbs 27:17). These relationships help shape us, build resilience, and remind us of who we are when life feels uncertain. But community is not just about encouragement—it's also about accountability. There's something powerful about sharing our struggles and victories with trusted friends or mentors. Opening up creates space for prayer, support, and mutual growth. As Paul wrote, *"Carry each other's burdens, and in this way you will fulfil the law of Christ"* (Galatians 6:2). When we're honest about where we are, others can stand with us, helping us to stay the course.

Being part of a wider faith community is also vital. Whether it's a local church, a small group, or a circle of like-minded believers, gathering with others renews our faith. It reminds us we're part of something bigger than ourselves. The book of Hebrews urges us, *"Let us consider how we may spur one another on toward love and good deeds, not giving up meeting together... but encouraging one another"* (Hebrews 10:24–25). There's strength in shared worship, prayer, and service— these are the places where miracles are often born.

Community brings perspective, strength, and the reminder that we are not alone. As we invest in healthy, faith-filled relationships, we find courage to keep going, even when the road is rough. Together, we reflect the body of Christ—many parts, one purpose, moving

5. Little Faith, Great Miracles in Action

Living with faith doesn't require perfection. It simply asks for belief—a willingness to trust God, even when we don't have all the answers. Little faith, when placed in a big God, can move mountains. The smallest seed of trust, nurtured through prayer, scripture, gratitude, and community, can yield life-changing miracles. As we learn to practise faith daily, face fear with truth, and lean into the unknown with hope, we begin to live from a place of trust instead of striving. Miracles don't always come as dramatic breakthroughs. Sometimes, they show up in the quiet peace that replaces anxiety, in the strength to take the next step, or in the unexpected provision just when we need it most. When we anchor our hearts in God's goodness and surround ourselves with others who call out the best in us, our faith grows—little by little. And in that space, God works. He meets us in the ordinary, transforms our perspective, and leads us into a life marked by grace, courage, and wonder.

PART III

EMBRACING THE PARADOX: BIG FAITH LITTLE RELIGION, LITTLE FAITH GREAT MIRACLES

BEYOND THE BOUNDARIES OF TRADITIONAL RELIGION, LIES THE POWER OF TRUE FAITH

As we continue this journey, we step into a new layer of exploration—one that invites us to hold tension with grace. We've seen how even the smallest seed of faith can unlock miracles. Now, we consider another layer of paradox: that deep, abiding faith can flourish beyond the confines of religious tradition, while even uncertain, trembling faith can still usher in the divine.

This part of the book draws together the threads we've been weaving through scriptural insights, and everyday moments of transformation, and takes them one step further. We begin to embrace the mystery, the contradiction, and the beauty of what it means to carry Big Faith in a world where religion often feels too small. And we wrestle with the wonder that even Little Faith—when placed in the right hands—can open the floodgates of Great Miracles.

The phrase Big Faith Little Religion speaks to a faith that is expansive, living, and deeply personal. It's not tied to ritual or rule but rooted in relationship—faith that listens, responds, and trusts without needing certainty. This kind of faith may sit outside the bounds of organised religion, yet it pulses with power.

Little Faith Great Miracles reminds us that faith doesn't need to be loud or flawless to move the hand of God. Even faith the size of a mustard seed can part seas, heal bodies, and mend hearts. This paradox humbles us. It draws us in. It tells the truth of a God who works not through perfection, but through presence. What follows is not a rejection of religion, but a reimagining of where and how faith can live. It's an invitation to go deeper—to trust more fully, even when we understand less. To believe that miracles are not reserved for the religious elite but are available to all who dare to hope.

As we move forward, may your heart stay open, your questions stay honest, and your faith—whether big or little—become the vessel through which God's grace flows.

Faith – The Unseen Force

Faith is one of the most enduring and deeply human experiences. For centuries, it has captured the attention of thinkers, theologians, and everyday seekers alike. At its heart, faith is not rooted in evidence or certainty. It's a deep trust—an unseen force—that anchors us to something beyond ourselves. This kind of trust doesn't rely on what can be measured or explained. It draws on conviction. Intuition. A quiet knowing that there is more to life than what our eyes can see or our minds can fully grasp. Faith invites us to step beyond the boundaries of logic and lean into something eternal. Philosopher William James once described faith as [1]"the willingness to act in a certain way without evidence, or even in the face of contrary evidence." That willingness—to risk, to trust, to believe when things are unclear—is what makes faith so transformative. It's not blind optimism, nor naïve hope. It's a bold posture of the heart, willing to walk forward even when the path is not fully lit.

Faith, by its very nature, holds tension. It asks us to live with mystery. To believe in something we cannot prove. And while that can feel unsettling, it also opens the door to wonder. When we stop demanding all the answers, we make space for divine surprises. Miracles. Breakthroughs. Encounters that don't fit into neat boxes but change us all the same.

The power of faith lies in its ability to carry us through uncertainty. It allows us to move—not because we have it all figured out, but because we trust the One who does. And in that trust, we begin to see: the unseen is not empty. It is full of grace, waiting to be discovered.

Faith as Trust and Confidence

At its core, faith is a deep trust and confidence in something beyond ourselves. This trust isn't rooted in empirical evidence or rational proof, but in conviction—an inward certainty that may defy logic yet carries great weight. Theologian Paul Tillich described faith as "the state of being ultimately concerned" (Tillich, 1957, p. 1) [2]. This concern is not just a matter of the mind or emotions; it is existential. It involves the whole person.

Faith is more than an idea we agree with or a feeling we chase. It shapes how we think, how we feel, and how we live. It becomes a lens through which we view the world and engage with it. Faith isn't passive belief—it's transformative. It changes how we walk through suffering, how we respond to uncertainty, and how we hope.

The Nature of Faith

Faith is not something that can be imposed or manufactured. It is a voluntary response—a conscious decision to place trust in what cannot be fully seen or explained. It isn't a static concept, nor is it confined to rigid definitions. Instead, faith unfolds gradually, shaped by the seasons of our lives. It matures in the tension between hope and uncertainty, becoming more resilient with every challenge we face.

Though often associated with religion, faith is not bound to religious structures. It is a deeply human experience, present in our relationships, aspirations, and even in our courage to begin again. We place faith in people, in promises, in new beginnings. We trust in the unseen potential of the future and sometimes in the healing of the present moment.

This kind of faith is not blind—it's brave. It holds space for doubt, yet chooses to trust anyway. It gives shape to how we interpret the world, how we love, and how we persevere. In this way, faith is not just belief—it is a way of being.

The Paradox of Faith

Faith lives in the tension between knowing and not knowing. It holds both conviction and uncertainty in the same breath. On one hand, faith provides the clarity and confidence to step forward—to believe in something beyond ourselves, and to pursue a purpose with intention and resolve. This conviction fuels our courage and gives direction to our lives.

Yet true faith also makes room for questions. It dares to lean into mystery, to trust when there is no clarity, and to continue when there is no proof. That very openness—so vulnerable and at times disorienting—is what allows faith to remain alive and growing. It does not shrink from doubt, but instead uses it as a doorway to deeper understanding.

This paradox is not a flaw in faith, but its strength. Faith is not a fixed destination but a continual unfolding. It matures in the space between bold assurance and quiet uncertainty, between revelation and silence. As we walk this path, we learn that faith does not require the absence of doubt, but the courage to keep walking with it. In embracing the tension, we become more open—more human—and more receptive to the transformative power of trust.

The Paradox of Faith and Doubt

Faith and doubt are not enemies—they are companions on the same road. While faith gives us the strength to believe, doubt invites us to examine what we believe. It challenges our assumptions, deepens our convictions, and keeps our spirituality honest. Without it, faith can settle into habit rather than remain a living, breathing force.

Doubt is not the absence of faith—it is the invitation to refine it. When we encounter questions we cannot answer or moments that shake us, it is often doubt that drives us to wrestle, reflect, and seek. And through that seeking, faith grows stronger, not weaker.

This tension is where faith becomes most alive. It isn't a rigid certainty that resists questions, but a posture of trust that continues even when everything isn't clear. Faith that has made space for doubt becomes more compassionate, more resilient, and more real. Instead of walking on shaky ground, we find ourselves standing on something deeper: a faith that has been tested, stretched, and shaped—not in spite of doubt, but through it.

The Interplay Between Faith and Doubt

Faith and doubt are not opposites—they are collaborators in the shaping of a deeper, more meaningful spirituality. Faith offers confidence and direction, while doubt brings depth and clarity. Together, they form a rhythm of belief that breathes and moves, evolving as we grow.

This interplay is vital for spiritual maturity. Without doubt, faith risks becoming brittle. Without faith, doubt has no anchor. But when the two coexist, they create a dynamic space where questions are welcome, and convictions are earned. This process invites us into a faith that is not simplistic, but rich with humility, resilience, and curiosity.

Embracing the Paradox of Faith and Doubt

To embrace both faith and doubt is to walk with open hands. It means resisting the urge for easy answers and allowing room for mystery. It calls for humility—a willingness to admit we don't have it all figured out—and the courage to keep seeking anyway.

This kind of faith doesn't shy away from tension. It leans in. It understands that spiritual depth isn't found in certainty alone, but in the quiet wrestling that happens in between. By accepting this paradox, we allow our faith to stretch, mature, and deepen. We become less concerned with having every answer, and more anchored in trust—trust that even in the questions, God is present.

The Paradox of Little Faith Great Miracles

One of the most beautiful paradoxes of faith is this: even the smallest seed of belief can yield the most extraordinary outcomes. It seems counterintuitive at first. We often assume that mountain-moving faith must be massive, unshakeable, and loud. But Jesus challenges that idea with a simple truth: *"If you have faith as small as a mustard seed, you*

*can say to this mountain, 'Move from here to there,' and it will move.
Nothing will be impossible for you.* " (Matthew 17:20) [3].

This isn't about quantity. It's about the nature of the seed. The mustard
seed, tiny and unassuming, contains within it the potential to grow into
something expansive and rooted. In the same way, faith—however
small—when sincere and alive, can open the way for miracles. The
power lies not in how much we believe, but in the *authenticity* of that
belief. Even a trembling yes can invite heaven into a situation. A
whispered prayer. A hesitant step forward. These, too, can be the soil
in which great miracles take root.

Big Faith Little Religion

Conversely, it's possible to hold great faith without being tightly bound
to religious formality. Faith and religion, though often intertwined, are
not interchangeable. Faith is personal. Intimate. It is the unseen trust
we carry in our hearts. Religion, meanwhile, is communal and
structured. It offers shared language, tradition, and rhythm.
One does not guarantee the other. You can be full of religious activity
and yet lack a living, trusting faith. And you can be far from pews and
pulpits, yet deeply rooted in the kind of faith that moves mountains.

This is the heart of the paradox: *Big faith doesn't always wear religious
robes.* And *little religion doesn't mean little faith.*

Still, there is value in both. When faith is personal and alive, and religion
is grounded in love rather than law, the two can complement each other.
Faith keeps religion from becoming hollow. Religion, when healthy, can
nurture and support faith.

The invitation is to find a balance. To cultivate a faith that is deep,
honest, and present in everyday life—and to engage in community not
out of obligation, but from a desire to walk alongside others in pursuit

of the sacred. When the heart of faith and the form of religion meet in harmony, something beautiful and enduring takes shape.

The Relationship Between Faith and Religion

The connection between faith and religion is not always straightforward. While the two are often linked, they are not the same. Faith is deeply personal—an inner trust, often intuitive and unseen. Religion, on the other hand, is communal and structured. It offers shared practices, sacred texts, rituals, and community.

Religion can provide a meaningful framework for spiritual growth. It helps us interpret life's questions, supports us in times of need, and gives us a sense of belonging. It can root faith in tradition, provide rhythm to spiritual life, and foster community through shared values and stories. But religion also carries the potential to limit. When reduced to rules, rituals, or rigid doctrine, it can become a system of control rather than an invitation to relationship. At its worst, religion can foster division, judgement, and fear.

Faith, by contrast, is not bound by formality. It's flexible and intimate. It can be nurtured through prayer, silence, Scripture, or liturgy—but also through nature, music, art, and everyday wonder. Faith can breathe freely outside of institutional walls.

For some, faith is deeply intertwined with religious practice. For others, it grows outside traditional frameworks altogether. What matters most is not where faith is expressed, but whether it is real—whether it is lived.

Faith does not require a steeple to be sacred. It only requires an open heart.

The Unseen Nature of Faith

Faith is often invisible. It does not announce itself in certainty or proof, but lives quietly in trust and hope. This is what makes it both powerful and mysterious. Faith dwells in the unseen, in the not-yet, in the space between what is known and what is longed for. As Hebrews reminds us, *"Now faith is the substance of things hoped for, the evidence of things not seen"* (Hebrews 11:1, KJV). [4]. Faith is not grounded in what we can prove or touch. It is grounded in what we trust to be true, even when there is no visible sign.

This makes faith difficult to define or quantify. It is not a formula. It doesn't fit into charts or measurements. It cannot be dissected in a lab. It is lived. Felt. Carried.

Faith is the courage to believe when nothing makes sense. The quiet strength to keep walking when the outcome is unclear. It is the soul's way of saying, "There is more," even when the evidence is not yet visible.

Though unseen, faith is not uncertain. It is not blind or naïve. It is rooted in relationship—with God, with mystery, with hope. It sees beyond what the eyes can grasp, and believes in what the heart knows to be real.

The Relationship Between Faith and Reason

Faith and reason have often been treated as rivals, as if belief and logic must stand on opposite shores. But the truth is more layered. Their relationship is not a battle between opposites, but a delicate and evolving dance—one that has shaped the way we make sense of the world for centuries. Søren Kierkegaard spoke of faith as a *"leap"*—a bold step beyond what reason can grasp (Kierkegaard, 1843, p. 55). [5] Faith, he argued, does not rest on proof. It is born in the space where certainty ends. Similarly, William James described faith as the courage to act even when evidence is lacking, or when the evidence seems to point the other way (James, 1902, p. 4). This kind of faith—raw, brave, and unprovable—is what opens us to transformation. And yet, faith is not irrational. It's not reckless or thoughtless. It is, in many ways, reason's counterpart. Where reason helps us analyse, faith helps us trust. Reason examines the seen; faith leans into the unseen. Together, they make a fuller kind of wisdom.

The Complementarity of Faith and Reason

Rather than seeing faith and reason as enemies, we can see them as companions. Reason helps us explore and articulate our beliefs; faith gives those beliefs depth, direction, and heart. Thomas Aquinas, one of the great Christian thinkers, taught that faith and reason are two ways of seeking truth. Faith builds the foundation. Reason helps us build upon it (Aquinas, 1274, p. 1). [6]

Faith asks us to trust. Reason helps us understand why that trust might be worth the risk. When both are present, they refine each other.

The Limits of Reason

But reason has its limits. It can take us far, but it cannot carry us across every threshold. Some things—the mystery of God, the purpose of suffering, the questions of eternity—stretch beyond the reach of logic. Immanuel Kant spoke of truths that lie beyond the bounds of human reason (Kant, 1781, p. 1).[7] These are not imaginary or irrelevant—they are simply too vast to be fully captured by the mind. This is where faith speaks. Not to replace reason, but to carry us where reason cannot go.

Faith gives us language for what cannot be explained. It gives us courage when answers fall short. And it invites us into a world where not everything has to be proven in order to be true.

The Role of Faith in Human Experience

Faith plays a vital role in shaping the human journey. It offers more than belief—it offers meaning. In the face of uncertainty, pain, or mystery, faith becomes a quiet anchor, grounding us in something greater than ourselves. It allows us to find purpose not just in the answers, but in the questions themselves.

When life presents complexities we cannot explain, or challenges we feel unequipped to face, faith gives us a way through. It invites us to trust—not blindly, but deeply. This trust does not ignore reason; it simply acknowledges that reason alone cannot hold the whole story. Faith helps us endure when facts fall short and empowers us to keep moving when nothing is certain.

Faith also provides a framework for resilience. In moments of struggle, faith calls forth courage. In moments of joy, it invites gratitude. Whether grounded in spiritual tradition or stirred by personal conviction, faith orients us toward hope—even when circumstances remain unresolved.

At its core, faith is an unseen force. It does not always operate on logic or evidence, yet it shapes how we live, love, and find our place in the world. It is not a rejection of reason, but a step beyond it—an embrace of something that cannot always be measured, but can still be known. In this way, faith remains one of the most powerful and enduring aspects of human experience.

THE ORIGINS OF FAITH AND WHAT INSPIRES IT

Faith is not born in a vacuum. It arises from a rich tapestry of human experience—shaped by personal moments, cultural surroundings, communal narratives, and spiritual practices. For some, faith springs from awe and wonder. For others, it's forged in crisis, whispered in silence, or inherited through generations. Whatever its entry point, faith finds root where the soul seeks meaning.

The Multifaceted Nature of Faith's Origins

Faith takes shape through a wide range of influences, making it both personal and universal. Philosopher and theologian John Hick describes faith as a response to a transcendent reality, one that is perceived and interpreted through the lens of human experience [1] (Hick, 1973, p. 12). Whether quiet or dramatic, these encounters with the sacred—however one defines that—create a foundation for belief and trust in something beyond ourselves. Personal experiences, in particular, are often powerful catalysts. A sudden recovery, a moment of unexpected peace, a sunset that stills the mind—these can stir a recognition of something larger at work. In moments of beauty, loss, gratitude or surrender, many find the beginnings of faith, or the deepening of it.

Culture, Community, and the Shaping of Belief

Our environment also helps shape the language and contours of faith. The household we grow up in, the stories we are told, and the rituals we practise all leave an imprint. For those raised in a religious home, faith may begin as tradition. For others, it emerges as a question— sometimes a resistance to dogma, or a yearning to belong to something not yet known. Culture offers the scaffolding upon which faith often builds: the symbols, scriptures, values, and voices that teach us how to relate to the divine—or why some choose not to. Even those who step away from inherited religion often carry traces of it, reimagining faith through their own experience of truth.

The Role of Spiritual Practice

Spiritual disciplines—such as prayer, contemplation, silence, or song— become the spaces where faith is nurtured. These practices offer rhythm to our spiritual lives, shaping our awareness and drawing our attention to the sacred. In stillness, we learn to listen. In repetition, we learn to trust. For many, it is not theology but daily practice that brings them closest to God. Spiritual practice also softens the grip of fear or doubt, not by removing life's complexities, but by reminding us we are not alone in them. Whether lighting a candle, walking in nature, or meditating on scripture, we create space for mystery to meet us—and faith is born again.

Experience as a Teacher of Faith

Ultimately, our lived experience becomes one of the greatest teachers of faith. It is through experience—joyful, painful, ordinary, or extraordinary—that we come to understand what we believe. Nature may awaken reverence. Loss may awaken trust. Love may awaken gratitude. These lived realities invite us into a faith that is not just taught but felt. Faith that arises from experience is often deeper than borrowed belief. It is faith that has been tested, stretched, and shaped by life itself. And because it is shaped by life, it remains alive—dynamic, evolving, and deeply human.

The Interplay Between Faith and Experience

Faith and experience are deeply intertwined. Our beliefs shape the way we see the world—what we notice, what we hold onto, what we hope for. At the same time, our lived experiences often become the soil in which faith is either planted, nurtured, or tested. Faith influences how we interpret life's events, and life's events, in turn, shape the contours of our faith. Philosopher Friedrich Nietzsche once suggested that faith is not merely an intellectual stance but a lived, felt commitment—one that engages our emotions and existential longings [2] (Nietzsche, 1883, p. 12). In this light, faith is less about abstract belief and more about how we make meaning in the face of the unknown. Experiences of love, loss, awe, injustice, or healing all have the power to shift us spiritually. A moment of kindness can deepen our belief in goodness. A season of suffering can stretch our capacity to trust. Our stories become the space where belief is tested, and sometimes, refined.

The Complexity of Faith's Origins

The roots of faith are rarely simple. They draw from personal encounters, cultural landscapes, and the spiritual frameworks we're surrounded by. Understanding these influences helps us appreciate that faith is not a static decision, but a lifelong unfolding.

Some discover faith in solitude; others awaken to it in moments of crisis or beauty. Some inherit it; others wrestle with it, reframe it, or find it in places far from where they began. The origins of faith are as diverse as humanity itself—woven into the complexities of personality, upbringing, and spiritual hunger.

Cultural and Social Influences

Culture shapes our language of faith. It gives us metaphors, sacred stories, communal rituals, and symbols that help us name what we feel and long for. As sociologist Emile Durkheim observed, religion—and by extension, much of faith—is often born from the shared beliefs of a community, embedded in social life [3]. (Durkheim, 1912, p. 10).

Whether raised in a Christian, Muslim, Hindu, Buddhist, or secular home, our early environments leave a mark. They can offer a foundation—or a challenge. A person taught the values of compassion and grace in a religious setting may carry these into adulthood as anchors of belief. Someone raised without formal religion may come to faith through questioning, longing, or spiritual exploration later in life.

The Role of Community in Shaping Faith

Community is one of the most powerful mirrors of faith. We rarely believe in isolation. Faith flourishes in connection—with others who reflect, affirm, challenge, or journey with us. As sociologist Peter Berger noted, the beliefs we hold are often reinforced—or re-examined—within the social networks we belong to (Berger, 1967, p. 15). Spiritual communities, in particular, can nurture faith through shared stories, acts of service, and collective worship. They provide spaces where doubt is held gently and encouragement is offered freely. In seasons of loss or joy, being surrounded by others who carry hope can reignite our own.

Even beyond formal religious settings, the power of relationships remains central. A friend who listens deeply, a mentor who speaks life into confusion, a stranger whose kindness reflects the divine—these encounters breathe life into belief.

Spiritual Practices and the Shaping of Faith

Spiritual practices—such as prayer, meditation, silence, or sacred ritual—have long been vehicles for nurturing and deepening faith. These disciplines create space for reflection, connection, and presence. They quiet the noise of daily life and reorient our attention towards something greater than ourselves.

Thomas Merton once wrote that contemplation does not simply remove us from the world, but instead anchors us more deeply in it [4]. (Merton, 1948, p. 12). In this way, practices like meditation or prayer don't merely cultivate peace—they foster trust. They give us language, rhythm, and posture for faith. Even in seasons of uncertainty, these habits tether us to hope.

Through repetition and intention, spiritual practices become more than habits; they become pathways. A breath prayer, a whispered Psalm, the lighting of a candle—each act grounds us in meaning and invites us to trust again.

The Role of Ritual in Faith Formation

Rituals have always held a sacred place in human spirituality. Whether it's the breaking of bread, the lighting of incense, or the laying on of hands, ritual has a way of rooting the invisible in the visible. It makes the unseen tangible.

Participating in ritual—whether in church, in nature, or in private devotion—allows the body to echo what the heart believes. It marks thresholds, honours memory, and anchors belief in the present moment. Rituals remind us that faith is not only something we think or feel, but something we enact with our whole being. The Eucharist, for example, is more than a symbolic act—it becomes a sacred encounter, a reminder of divine nearness. In moments like these, ritual becomes a vessel through which faith is both expressed and strengthened.

Nature as a Catalyst for Faith

For many, faith is awakened not in a sanctuary, but under the open sky. The majesty of mountains, the stillness of a forest, or the rhythm of ocean waves can stir something deep within—a quiet knowing that we are part of something vast and holy.

Thomas Berry spoke of the natural world as a revelation of the divine. (Berry, 1973, p. 10). Nature speaks in colour, texture, and scale—and when we pay attention, it invites awe. In such moments, faith does not arrive as a doctrine, but as a breathless awareness: we are not alone. Spending time in nature can evoke reverence. It can restore wonder. It can reframe our perspective and invite us into a deeper trust—one not built on certainty, but on stillness and surrender.

Awe and the Awakening of Trust

Awe and wonder are powerful seeds of faith. These experiences catch us off guard, open our hearts, and disarm our cynicism. They don't require a creed; they simply require our attention. A sky painted in sunset colours, a newborn's first cry, a moment of deep stillness—such encounters have the power to reawaken something within us. Awe reminds us that we are part of a mystery that can't be measured. It humbles us, and at the same time, lifts us. These moments are not only emotional—they are formative. They shape the way we relate to the world and to the divine. And though fleeting, they often leave a permanent mark on the soul.

Personal Experience and the Birth of Belief

Faith is **often** born in the hidden places—during moments we didn't plan or fully understand. A healing we can't explain. A comfort we feel in the middle of grief. A sense of being held when everything is falling apart. These deeply personal encounters become the roots of belief. They remind us that faith is not always taught—it is often experienced. For some, it begins in crisis; for others, in joy. But regardless of how it begins, these experiences shape our understanding of the sacred. They leave us changed, humbled, and often searching. And in that searching, faith is not only kindled—it grows.

Cultural and Social Influences on Faith

Faith does not arise in isolation. From the moment we are born, we are shaped by the traditions, customs, and beliefs of the communities we inhabit. Cultural heritage often provides the first language of faith—whether through sacred rituals, familiar prayers, or the rhythm of religious holidays observed in the home. These traditions offer a sense of continuity, connecting us to generations past and grounding us in identity. For someone raised in a particular religious environment, faith may feel instinctive—woven into the fabric of family life. Similarly, social influences such as friends, teachers, and spiritual mentors can reinforce and deepen one's beliefs, especially when they offer a consistent and supportive witness to that faith. Communities of faith don't just preserve belief—they shape it. They offer belonging, reinforce values, and provide the spiritual scaffolding upon which personal convictions can grow.

Spiritual Practices and the Inner Landscape

While culture and community provide context, spiritual practices cultivate the interior life of faith. Practices like prayer, meditation, worship, or sacred ritual help orient the heart and mind towards the divine. They create space for encounter, reflection, and renewal. Over time, these practices form a rhythm that anchors us. A quiet prayer before dawn, a moment of stillness under a tree, a shared meal of remembrance—all these are acts that shape the soul. They bring us back to what is eternal. Through them, we learn to listen differently. We become attentive not only to the divine, but also to ourselves. Faith, then, becomes not something we simply inherit, but something we practise—something we live.

Nature as a Window to the Divine

For many, nature is the first sanctuary. Its grandeur and intricacy stir something deep within. Mountains seem to hold ancient wisdom. The sea speaks in mystery. Forests invite stillness. In these places, words fall away. What remains is presence. The beauty of the natural world often inspires reverence, reminding us of the vastness of creation and the fragility of our place within it. It lifts our gaze beyond the ordinary and draws us into silent wonder. Such encounters with nature can awaken faith—not in a theological sense, but in the soul's sense of connection. They remind us that faith doesn't always need structure. Sometimes, it begins with awe.

Personal Encounters with the Divine

And yet, for some, faith arrives not through tradition or nature, but through a direct encounter with the sacred. These moments are often unplanned, unexplainable, and unforgettable. It might be a moment of divine presence in a hospital room. A sudden awareness of being held in grief. A vision, a whisper, a profound inner knowing. These experiences don't always come with explanations, but they leave us changed—awakened to something greater. Such encounters often become turning points. They mark the beginning of a journey or deepen one already underway. They bring clarity, purpose, and direction. And though others may struggle to understand them, the one who experienced it knows: something holy happened here.

Understanding the Origins of Faith

To truly appreciate the role of faith in our lives, we must first understand where it comes from. Faith does not arise from a single source. It emerges through experience, tradition, practice, and encounter. It is shaped by the stories we inherit, the questions we wrestle with, the silence we sit in, and the moments that stir something beyond explanation. By exploring the origins of faith—whether personal, cultural, spiritual, or natural—we develop not only a deeper understanding of our own journey but also a greater respect for the diverse paths others walk. In doing so, we move away from judgement and into curiosity, away from assumption and into reverence. Faith, in all its forms, is a window into the mystery of being human. It invites us to see ourselves not as isolated individuals, but as part of a greater story—interconnected, unfolding, sacred.

The Power of Faith

Faith holds quiet power. It does not always arrive with answers, but it gives us the courage to live with questions. It inspires resilience in hardship, hope in uncertainty, and wonder in the face of mystery. Whether rooted in personal experience, community tradition, sacred practice, or an encounter with beauty or the divine, faith becomes a force that grounds and guides us. It transforms how we see, how we act, and how we love. To honour faith is to honour the deeply human longing for meaning, connection, and transcendence. It is to recognise that within each person, regardless of belief system or background, lies a sacred search for what is true, good, and eternal.

By embracing the diversity and depth of faith, we become not only more spiritually awake—but more fully alive.

THE MULTIFACETED NATURE OF FAITH ORIGINS

Faith doesn't begin in the same place for everyone. It rises from different sources—personal experiences, cultural traditions, social environments, and spiritual practices. Its roots run deep, drawing nourishment from the stories we live, the questions we ask, and the moments that shape us. John Hick described faith as a response to a transcendent reality, one that reveals itself through the layers of human experience [1] (Hick, 1973, p. 12). These layers can be emotional or intellectual, inherited or discovered. Understanding this diversity helps us appreciate that faith is not one-size-fits-all—it is deeply personal and always evolving.

Personal Experiences and the Awakening of Faith

Many people first encounter faith through personal experience. These moments can come unexpectedly—a brush with mortality, the loss of a loved one, a miraculous recovery, or a sudden awareness of something greater. In these moments, we begin to ask different questions, searching for meaning that goes beyond the surface. Evelyn Underhill referred to such experiences as encounters with the divine—sacred interruptions that stir the soul and reorient the heart[2] (Underhill, 1911, p. 23). For Viktor Frankl, suffering itself could be a crucible for faith, compelling us to reach for hope when everything else falls away [3]. (Frankl, 1946, p. 12). These deeply personal moments can mark the beginning of a faith that is not simply adopted but lived.

The Influence of Culture and Community

Our cultural background often becomes the first soil in which faith is planted. Religious traditions passed down through families, festivals, language, and customs create a framework for understanding the world and our place in it. Emile Durkheim noted that religion and culture are tightly woven, offering a shared structure for interpreting life's biggest questions [4]. (Durkheim, 1912, p. 10). Alongside this, our social relationships matter. Peter Berger observed how community can affirm belief by creating a space where faith is practised together and made visible in everyday life [5] (Berger, 1967, p. 15). Being part of a faith community doesn't just shape what we believe—it reminds us that we do not walk alone.

Spiritual Practices That Nourish Faith

Practices like prayer, meditation, silence, and ritual are not merely habits—they are encounters. Thomas Merton suggested that these disciplines open the soul to what cannot be seen but is deeply felt [6] (Merton, 1948, p. 12). They give us language for what we sense but cannot explain, and they anchor us in the mystery of something beyond ourselves. In stillness, we hear what busyness often drowns out. In ritual, we embody sacred truths. These practices don't impose belief; they make space for belief to emerge, settle, and grow.

Nature: The Sacred in the Everyday

The natural world has long stirred the soul toward wonder. Mountains, oceans, and forests speak of a grandeur that transcends words. As Thomas Berry observed, nature's intricate beauty and scale can evoke a reverence that becomes a form of worship [7] (Berry, 1973, p. 10). For many, time spent in nature is not just restorative but spiritual. It reminds us of our smallness in the best way—realigning us with something greater and drawing us into a deeper sense of belonging to the whole of creation.

Embracing the Origins of Faith

Faith does not arrive in one shape or form. It comes through beauty and grief, culture and silence, tradition and transcendence. Sometimes it is inherited. Other times it is fought for. But always, it is deeply human. By embracing the diverse origins of faith, we develop more than understanding—we cultivate empathy. We begin to see that no two spiritual journeys are the same, but each is worthy of honour. In that space, we find unity not through sameness, but through shared longing—for truth, for meaning, for something beyond ourselves.

FAITH WITHOUT WORKS IS DEAD – THE IMPORTANCE OF ACTION

Faith, at its core, is not passive. It is not merely a feeling or an idea, but a force that moves us—calling us to act, to serve, to build, to give. While belief may begin within the heart, it must eventually find its way into the hands and feet. As the letter of James so plainly puts it, "Faith without works is dead" (James 2:26, KJV). Without expression, faith becomes hollow—like a well with no water.

The Living Tension Between Faith and Works

There is often a tension between faith and works, as though they belong to different realms—one spiritual, the other practical. But in truth, they are intertwined. Faith may be the root, but works are the fruit. Belief gives direction; action gives proof. James challenges the idea that faith can be separated from how we live. "Show me your faith without works," he writes, "and I will show you my faith by my works" (James 2:18, KJV). In this, he invites us to understand that true faith will always lead to some form of action—not as an obligation, but as a natural outflow.

When Faith Moves Us

Faith becomes real when it moves us—when it shifts our priorities, changes our choices, and motivates us to love beyond convenience. A belief in justice becomes visible in advocacy. A belief in mercy is revealed through forgiveness. A belief in compassion is expressed in kindness and care. Consider someone who believes in the dignity of all people. That conviction, left unexpressed, changes little. But when it compels them to stand against injustice, to speak up for the voiceless, or to serve the marginalised, faith comes alive. Faith without expression remains invisible. It is action that gives it shape.

The Reciprocal Dance of Faith and Practice

The relationship between belief and behaviour is not one-directional. As much as faith inspires works, our works also shape and strengthen our faith. When we choose to live what we believe—however imperfectly—we often find that faith grows stronger in the doing. A person who believes in the power of prayer might begin with discipline, praying daily even when they feel nothing. Over time, the practice begins to bear fruit. Moments of peace emerge. Insights surface. Trust deepens. The act of living the faith becomes the means by which faith is reinforced. This reciprocity is vital. Practice strengthens belief. Action cultivates conviction. And what began as a quiet trust matures into a living testimony.

A Faith That Shows

Works are not about proving something to others or earning spiritual approval—they are about integrity. They are the outward reflection of an inward reality. When our actions align with our convictions, we live with wholeness. When they don't, we experience dissonance. Faith that never leaves the realm of thought is incomplete. It must spill over into how we love, serve, forgive, speak, spend, build, and share. That is the kind of faith that not only transforms us—but begins to transform the world around us.

The Story of the Blind Man at the Pool of Siloam

One of the most vivid examples of faith expressed through action is found in the Gospel of John—the healing of the man born blind at the Pool of Siloam (John 9:1–38, KJV). This story is not just about physical sight restored but also about spiritual insight gained through obedience, trust, and the courage to act. A Little Faith, a Great Miracle.

A Blind Man, a Question, and a Purpose

As Jesus and His disciples passed by, they noticed a man who had been blind from birth. The disciples asked, "Master, who did sin, this man, or his parents, that he was born blind?" (John 9:2, KJV). Their question revealed a common assumption—that suffering must be the result of personal sin. But Jesus reframed the moment: "Neither hath this man sinned, nor his parents: but that the works of God should be made manifest in him" (John 9:3, KJV). In that moment, Jesus shifted the focus from blame to purpose. The man's blindness was not a punishment but an opportunity—for divine power to be revealed and faith to be awakened.

The Act of Obedience

Rather than healing the man instantly, Jesus spat on the ground, made clay, anointed the man's eyes, and gave a peculiar instruction: "Go, wash in the pool of Siloam" (John 9:7, KJV). The man did as he was told. He could have questioned the method. He could have dismissed the command. But instead, he obeyed—and that obedience became the doorway to his healing. As he washed in the waters of Siloam, his eyes were opened. He returned, seeing. What began as a physical miracle soon became a journey of spiritual awakening.

Faith That Walks Before It Sees

The power of this story lies in what happened between the command and the miracle. The man walked to the pool while still blind. He acted on faith, not certainty. He obeyed before he had any proof that healing would come. It was not just belief that healed him—it was belief expressed in movement. Faith often requires us to act before we understand, to step out before we see the result. The man's healing reminds us that miracles are often unlocked through ordinary acts of obedience.

Trust Beyond the Unknown

What makes the man's faith remarkable is not just his obedience, but his trust. He had never seen Jesus. He had no guarantee of healing. And yet, he trusted the voice that gave the command. This kind of trust is not rooted in evidence but in encounter. It is the kind of trust that says, "Even if I don't know the outcome, I will take the next step." And in taking that step, the man found not only physical sight, but eventually spiritual revelation.

Other Examples of Faith in Action

Faith is not a static idea or a fleeting emotion—it is a living force that expresses itself through our choices, our obedience, and our courage. Throughout scripture, we encounter men and women whose actions were shaped by faith. Their stories remind us that true belief moves us to act, even in uncertainty, and often against the odds.

Mother Teresa's Ministry: A Life of Selfless Service

One of the most compelling modern-day examples of faith in action is found in the life of Mother Teresa. Her unwavering dedication to the poor, sick, and forgotten stands as a powerful testimony to the depth of faith expressed through compassion and service. In every act of mercy, she showed that faith is not something we merely believe—it is something we live.

A Faith Lived Through Service

Mother Teresa's ministry in the slums of Calcutta was marked by her relentless commitment to the most vulnerable. She established homes, orphanages, and clinics, often with limited resources, but an abundance of love. Her faith propelled her to care for those the world had cast aside—not only attending to physical needs, but also offering emotional comfort and spiritual presence. What set her apart was not the scale of her ministry, but the sincerity of her heart. She did not seek fame or applause; she sought to love as Christ loved. She listened. She wept. She stood beside the dying with the same reverence as she would before a king. Her life embodied the gospel's call to love "the least of these" (Matthew 25:40, KJV).

Faith That Transforms

The impact of Mother Teresa's ministry cannot be measured by numbers alone. Her example reshaped how many Christians understood faith— not as private devotion alone, but as public, hands-on love. She reminded the world that true faith challenges complacency, crosses social barriers, and gives without expecting anything in return. Her actions spoke louder than sermons. She made the love of God visible, touching lives that others overlooked. Through her, many saw faith not as lofty theology, but as simple acts of kindness that bring dignity to the human soul.

A Lasting Legacy

Mother Teresa's legacy endures—not in monuments or titles, but in every person inspired to serve, to love, and to see Christ in the eyes of the suffering. Her life reminds us that faith doesn't sit still. It moves. It reaches. It bends low. And in doing so, it lifts others up. She left behind more than an example—she left a call. A call to believe with our hearts and serve with our hands. A call to live out our convictions in ways that heal, restore, and affirm the value of every human life.

Faith Expressed Through Deeds

The lives of David, Rahab, Abraham, the Good Samaritan, and Mother Teresa all echo the same truth: real faith always moves toward action. It listens, it sees, and it responds. It's not measured by words alone, but by how we show up for others—especially those who cannot repay us. We are not called to heroic acts for recognition, but to quiet, daily acts of love that reflect the heart of Christ. To be the hands and feet of Jesus is to embody His compassion, not just in what we say, but in how we live. As we reflect on these examples, we are invited to consider: what does faith look like in our own lives? Where can we step out, reach out, and show up—not just in belief, but in action?

The Importance of Action in Faith

Faith is not complete without action. It is through our actions that our faith becomes visible, tangible, and transformative. True faith is not passive or abstract—it is a lived reality. When we act on what we believe, we demonstrate our commitment to our values, and we give our faith depth and substance. As James reminds us, *"Faith without works is dead"* (James 2:26, KJV). This verse doesn't diminish the power of belief; rather, it emphasises that belief alone is not enough. Without action, our faith remains theoretical. But when we live it out, we move from words to witness, from intention to impact.

Action Builds Trust

Putting faith into action also cultivates trust. Trust in God. Trust in others. Trust in ourselves. As we step forward, even when the path is uncertain, we practise reliance on something greater than our understanding. Proverbs puts it plainly: *"Trust in the Lord with all thine heart; and lean not unto thine own understanding"* (Proverbs 3:5, KJV). This kind of trust isn't blind—it's bold. It is trust that moves us forward, even when we cannot see the full picture. Taking action from a place of faith also builds internal confidence. Each step reinforces our commitment and increases our capacity to believe again. We begin to experience a faith that is both tested and strengthened through lived experience.

The Transformative Power of Faith in Action

Faith expressed through action is powerful—it transforms us and those around us. When we serve, love, give, or stand for justice because of our faith, we become part of something larger. We don't just talk about the gospel; we live it. As Paul writes, *"Faith comes by hearing, and hearing by the word of God"* (Romans 10:17, KJV). But hearing alone is not the end. Faith matures through response—through obedience, risk, and service. Each act becomes a declaration: I believe, and I will act accordingly. From the blind man at the Pool of Siloam to the courage of Abraham, the compassion of the Good Samaritan, and the lifelong service of Mother Teresa, we see this truth played out. Their faith wasn't confined to belief. It moved them—literally and spiritually.

THE INSEPARABILITY OF FAITH AND WORKS

Faith is not merely a feeling or intellectual conviction—it is meant to be lived. True faith finds its expression in action. As James puts it plainly, *"Faith without works is dead"[1].* (James 2:26, KJV). This powerful truth reminds us that belief alone is not enough. Faith must move beyond words and feelings. It must be visible in how we live.

The Importance of Living Out Our Beliefs

When we act in alignment with our faith, we not only demonstrate personal integrity but become a living testimony to what we believe. As Dietrich Bonhoeffer once said, *"Faith is the beginning of a new life—a life that is not just a matter of personal piety, but a life that is lived out in the world"* [2] (Bonhoeffer, 1955, p. 15). Authentic faith moves us outward. It cannot be confined to private belief but is revealed through public action.

Authenticity and Integrity

Living out our faith requires both authenticity and integrity. When our actions mirror our convictions, we demonstrate a faith that is trustworthy and grounded. Jesus urged his followers to let their lives reflect God's light: *"Let your light so shine before men, that they may see your good works, and glorify your Father which is in heaven"*(Matthew 5:16, KJV). This is more than moral behaviour—it is faith embodied in kindness, justice, humility, and love.

A Caution on Misguided Movements

Not all teachings that emphasise belief and action are rooted in a healthy understanding of faith. In fact, some movements have distorted the relationship between faith, confession, and results—leading many into confusion and even despair.

The Confession Principle Movement

In the late 1980s and early 1990s, the Confession Principle Movement—closely linked to the Word of Faith tradition—encouraged believers to speak their desires into reality, claiming biblical support from verses like *"The tongue has the power of life and death"* (Proverbs 18:21, NIV). While this teaching initially appeared empowering, it often reduced faith to a formula and made the believer solely responsible for outcomes. When prayers went unanswered or "confessions" failed, many were left feeling ashamed, guilty, or spiritually inadequate.

The Law of Attraction

This secular cousin of the Confession Principle gained popularity through books like *The Secret* by Rhonda Byrne. It promoted the idea that focused thinking and visualisation could attract health, wealth, and success. But like its Christian counterpart, it placed the entire burden of success on the individual, ignoring external realities like suffering, injustice, and providence. As Barbara Ehrenreich observed, *"The Law of Attraction is a form of magical thinking which can be damaging, because it ignores the role of chance, luck, and circumstance in our lives."*

The Law of Assumption

Neville Goddard's teachings on the Law of Assumption pushed this idea further, claiming that we manifest reality through the assumptions we carry. It called for a deep inner conviction—not just spoken words or positive thoughts. While this sounds more nuanced, it still risks placing spiritual pressure on the individual rather than fostering true faith in God's sovereignty. As Gregg Braden explained, *"The power of assumption is not just about thinking positive thoughts; it's about embodying a new reality with every fibre of our being."*

A More Grounded Faith

These movements, though influential, often overlook the mystery, complexity, and grace woven into our spiritual lives. They fail to account for suffering, divine timing, or the communal nature of faith. A mature and biblically rooted faith recognises that while our words and beliefs do matter, they are not magic spells. Faith is not about control—it's about surrender, trust, obedience, and consistent action aligned with the heart of God.

Bearing Witness Through Action

Living out our faith is not only about personal growth—it's about witness. Theologian Karl Barth wrote, *"The Christian community is the community of those who are called to bear witness to the Gospel"[3]* (Barth, 1936, p. 12). When our lives reflect the love, justice, and mercy of Christ, we draw others to the source of our hope—not through persuasion, but through presence.

Inspiring Others

Living out our beliefs can inspire others to reflect on their own spiritual journeys. When we demonstrate a genuine and consistent commitment to our values, we create a ripple effect—one that invites others to question, explore, and perhaps even reimagine their own relationship with faith. Our lives become a quiet testimony, not through perfection, but through authenticity, kindness, and perseverance.

As the apostle Paul writes, *"Let your conversation be always full of grace, seasoned with salt, so that you may know how to answer everyone"*. (Colossians 4:6, NIV). This call is not merely about the words we use, but the tone and spirit behind them. A life seasoned with grace is magnetic—it softens hearts, opens doors, and makes room for questions to be asked without fear of judgement. Whether it's through acts of kindness, quiet resilience in hardship, or integrity in everyday decisions, faith in action has the power to awaken something deep in others. It shows that spirituality is not a set of abstract beliefs, but a way of being in the world. When people see that our faith leads us to live with compassion, humility, and hope, they are more likely to ask what sustains us—and in that moment, we have the privilege of pointing them to the source of our strength. In this way, our faith becomes not only a light for our own path, but a lantern for others walking through uncertainty, showing them that there is a way forward—a way marked by love, truth, and grace.

The Relationship Between Faith and Works in Christian Theology

In Christian theology, the relationship between faith and works has long been a foundational—and at times, contentious—discussion. The Protestant reformer Martin Luther famously championed *sola fide*, or "faith alone", as the means by which a person is justified before God [4] (Luther, 1520). For Luther, salvation could not be earned through human effort, but was received by grace through faith. In contrast, the Catholic tradition has upheld the importance of both *fides et opera*—faith and works—as integral to the life of salvation [5] (Catechism of the Catholic Church, 1992). Good works, such as acts of charity, compassion, and service, are not seen as earning salvation but as the fruit and fulfilment of living faith. Despite their theological differences, both traditions affirm a vital truth: faith, if genuine, will be lived out. It cannot remain static or hidden. As Alister McGrath explains, *"Faith is not simply a matter of intellectual assent, but is expressed in acts of charity, compassion, and service"* [6] (McGrath, 2005, p. 12). In other words, real faith reveals itself through real-life choices.

The Importance of Works in Demonstrating Faith

James, the biblical writer, underscores this with unmistakable clarity: *"Faith without works is dead"* (James 2:26, KJV). His message is not that works replace faith, but that they prove it. Works become the visible sign of an inner conviction. As he boldly states, *"Show me your faith without your works, and I will show you my faith by my works"* (James 2:18, NKJV). In this way, works are not an alternative to faith but a demonstration of it. They reflect the integrity of our beliefs, anchoring them in tangible action. Whether through serving others, caring for the vulnerable, or living with integrity and compassion, our works give flesh to the faith we profess. Rather than being in opposition, faith and works together form a rhythm—one that moves belief from theory into practice, and transforms theology into lived witness. In the Christian life, the two are not competitors but companions.

The Intersection of Faith and Works in Christian Living

The relationship between faith and works has long been a central theme in Christian thought, stirring reflection, debate, and at times, division. Martin Luther's call to *sola fide*—faith alone—became a cornerstone of Protestant theology, asserting that salvation is a gift of grace received through faith, not earned through deeds, (Luther, 1520). Meanwhile, the Catholic tradition has long held that *fides et opera*—faith and works— together reflect the fullness of a believer's response to God. (Catechism of the Catholic Church, 1992). Despite their theological nuances, both traditions arrive at a shared truth: real faith must be lived. It cannot remain abstract or internal. As Alister McGrath puts it, *"Faith is not simply a matter of intellectual assent, but is expressed in acts of charity, compassion, and service"*. (McGrath, 2005, p. 12). The epistle of James affirms this plainly: *"Faith without works is dead"* (James 2:26, KJV).

Works as the Evidence of Authentic Faith

Works do not replace faith—they reveal it. They become the outward evidence of an inward conviction. James challenges us, *"Show me your faith without your works, and I will show you my faith by my works"* (James 2:18, NKJV). In this, he calls for integrity between belief and behaviour—a life where what we say we believe is mirrored by how we live. Faith without expression can become inert. But faith that leads to action becomes transformational—not only for the individual, but for the community around them. The Christian life, then, is not just defined by what we believe, but by how those beliefs shape our habits, relationships, and decisions.

Faith in Practice: A Lived Theology

Theologian N.T. Wright echoes this, writing, *"The Christian life is not just about having the right beliefs, but about living out those beliefs in practical ways"[7]* (Wright, 2009, p. 15). Theology must become lived theology. In a world aching for integrity, faith that moves the hands as well as the heart becomes a powerful witness. This does not mean we earn salvation through our deeds, but that our deeds testify to the faith already alive within us. Whether through compassion, service, generosity, or quiet acts of mercy, the expression of faith is found in the rhythms of daily life. It is found in how we love, serve, forgive, and give.

A Call to Integrated Living

The relationship between faith and works is not merely a theological puzzle; it is an invitation. It asks us to reflect on the alignment between what we profess and how we live. When faith and works walk hand in hand, we begin to embody the gospel—not just believe it. May we be the kind of people whose lives echo what our lips proclaim. May our faith not remain dormant or disembodied, but be made real through acts of grace, humility, and love. In doing so, we not only deepen our own spiritual journey but become part of God's healing presence in the world.

THE ROLE OF WORKS IN DEMONSTRATING FAITH

Faith was never meant to remain invisible. It moves, it acts, and it leaves traces wherever it goes. Our works—what we do with our hands, our time, our influence—are not the root of our faith, but they are the fruit. They reveal what is unseen in the heart and make it visible to the world around us. Jesus taught this plainly: *"Let your light so shine before men, that they may see your good works, and glorify your Father which is in heaven"* [1] (Matthew 5:16, KJV). In this, we see that good works are not about self-promotion, but about witness. They serve as reflections of God's love, drawing others toward His light.

Faith Expressed Visibly

Our actions speak long before we ever open our mouths. Acts of compassion, service, generosity, and justice become the language of faith in a world often deaf to religious words. As James reminds us, *"Faith without works is dead"* [2] (James 2:26, KJV). It's not that works save us—but they confirm and complete the faith we profess. Belief and action were never meant to be separated. Theologian N.T. Wright puts it clearly: *"The Christian life is not just about having the right beliefs, but about living out those beliefs in practical ways"* [3] (Wright, 2009, p. 15). Faith that doesn't translate into movement—into something lived—misses its purpose.

Inspiring Others Through Our Actions

Works born from faith don't just affirm our convictions; they awaken something in others. When we act in love, mercy, or justice, our lives become a visible testimony—sparking curiosity, stirring hope, and sometimes even inspiring change. As we live out what we believe, we give others permission to do the same. Our lives become a kind of lighthouse, offering direction in a world full of fog.

Wilberforce: A Legacy of Faith-Fuelled Action

One of the most compelling historical examples of faith in action is William Wilberforce, the British politician who led the charge against the transatlantic slave trade. Wilberforce's Christianity wasn't abstract or confined to private belief—it was the fire that fuelled his fight for justice. He saw every human being as carrying the image of God, and this conviction made slavery intolerable to him. Despite facing fierce opposition, social ridicule, and multiple defeats in Parliament, Wilberforce pressed on. His tireless campaigning eventually led to the passing of the Slave Trade Act of 1807 and later, the Slavery Abolition Act of 1833—just days before his death.

Wilberforce's story is more than a political victory; it is a profound testament to what can happen when faith is carried into public life. His activism was not driven by ideology alone, but by a gospel-rooted vision of human dignity. He believed that faith had to move beyond pews and private prayers—it had to confront systems of oppression and speak on behalf of the voiceless. His legacy reminds us that faith is not passive. It is not neutral in the face of injustice. True faith steps in, speaks up, and presses forward. As we reflect on Wilberforce's courage, we are invited to examine our own lives: How is my faith visible? What injustice breaks my heart—and what might God be calling me to do about it?

Summary

Works are not an optional extra to faith—they are its evidence. Through what we do, we give shape to what we believe. Whether in quiet acts of kindness or bold stands for justice, our faith becomes visible and real. As we consider the lives of those who have gone before us—whether biblical figures, modern saints, or ordinary believers—we are reminded that faith must move. May we, too, be stirred to live out what we profess, allowing our daily choices to reflect our deepest convictions. In doing so, we do more than live faithfully—we leave behind a trail of grace that others can follow.

THE IMPORTANCE OF AUTHENTICITY IN FAITH AND WORKS

Authenticity is the heartbeat of genuine faith. It goes beyond what we say we believe and reaches into how we live, love, and serve. When our faith is real, it becomes visible—lived out in ways that reflect conviction, not convenience. As Karl Barth reminds us, "Faith is not a matter of intellectual assent or emotional feeling, but a matter of obedience and action" [1] (Barth, 1936, p. 15).

Why Authenticity Matters

True faith must be rooted in conviction, not appearance. When our beliefs are heartfelt and sincere, they will naturally flow into action. It's this alignment—between what we believe and how we behave—that builds trust and reveals integrity. Authenticity ensures our spiritual life is not just a performance, but a practice. Without authenticity, faith becomes hollow. When our words and actions drift apart, we risk sounding hypocritical. Others can sense the disconnection. And over time, we ourselves begin to feel unanchored—disconnected not only from others but from God. This leads to spiritual fatigue and even disillusionment. A life that merely performs belief without living it becomes a life of burnout and frustration.

The Consequences of Inauthentic Faith

Inauthentic faith erodes credibility. When what we profess doesn't match how we live, it not only damages our witness but can also create a sense of spiritual estrangement. The motions of faith become mechanical. Instead of being shaped by truth, we end up trapped by pretence. Worse still, inauthenticity blocks transformation. Superficial belief may tick boxes, but it doesn't change hearts. Growth requires honesty. Without it, we are left repeating religious rituals that no longer stir the soul.

Cultivating Authenticity

How, then, do we keep our faith authentic? It begins with self-reflection—a willingness to examine our motives, ask hard questions, and identify where our actions may not yet match our convictions. It requires courage to admit where we are falling short, but such honesty is the ground from which real growth can emerge. It also calls for vulnerability. Genuine connection—with God and with others—depends on our willingness to be seen as we truly are. Vulnerability invites trust. It builds bridges. It opens the door to deeper relationships where we are not hiding behind performance, but showing up with integrity.

As we nurture authenticity, we find our faith becoming not just something we talk about, but something we live—something others can see and feel.

Authenticity is not an accessory to faith—it is its foundation. When our words and actions align, when our beliefs are lived with honesty and conviction, faith becomes transformative. It shapes not only our own lives but leaves a mark on those around us. In a world weary of pretense, authentic faith stands out. And it invites others to seek something real.

The Interdependence of Faith and Works

Faith without works is dead, and works without faith are empty. The relationship between the two is not linear but deeply intertwined—each giving life and meaning to the other. True faith must move beyond belief into action, while meaningful works must flow from conviction rather than mere duty.

A Dynamic Partnership

This paradox lies at the heart of Christian life. As James writes, "Faith without works is dead" [2] (James 2:26, KJV). Faith alone, unexpressed, becomes stagnant. Yet works done without the anchor of faith can become performative—driven by appearances or obligation rather than transformation. Together, faith and works form a dynamic partnership: one inspires, the other manifests.

A Life Lived Outward

Genuine faith expresses itself in visible, practical ways. It compels us to live with purpose and integrity. As Dietrich Bonhoeffer observed, "Faith is the beginning of a new life, a life that is not just a matter of personal piety, but a life that is lived out in the world" [3] (Bonhoeffer, 1955, p. 15). When faith is real, it reaches outward—it shapes how we serve, love, and show up for others.

A Witness to the World

When our faith is lived with sincerity and humility, it becomes a witness. People don't just hear our beliefs—they see them. As Jesus said, "Let your light shine before men, that they may see your good works and glorify your Father in heaven"[4] (Matthew 5:16, KJV). Authentic faith has a ripple effect. It inspires. It reveals the character of the One we trust. And it reminds the world that hope is still alive.

Summary

Faith and works are not opposing ideas—they are inseparable expressions of a life surrendered to God. Real faith moves us. Real works reveal Him. When we live with both sincerity and action, we don't just honour our values—we light the way for others to do the same.

WORKS OF FAITH WITH ONLY LITTLE RELIGION

What does it mean to live out our faith in a world where religion can sometimes feel rigid, outdated, or restrictive? In this chapter, we explore how a deep and dynamic faith can remain alive—even flourish—outside the confines of institutional religion. This is not about discarding tradition, but about distinguishing between the framework of religion and the living pulse of faith.

Living Beyond the Boundaries

Living out faith beyond religious boundaries requires clarity and courage. Religion, at its best, offers rhythm, reflection, and a sense of belonging. But when it becomes entangled in legalism or cultural baggage, it can cloud the essence of faith. As Paul Tillich wisely noted, "Faith is not a matter of intellectual assent or emotional feeling, but a matter of ultimate concern" [1] (Tillich, 1957, p. 12). True faith reaches beyond custom—it speaks to what truly matters. Jesus addressed this tension directly. "The Sabbath was made for man, not man for the Sabbath" [2] (Mark 2:27, KJV). In other words, faith was never meant to serve rules—rules were meant to serve faith. When rituals eclipse relationship, religion becomes an obstacle rather than a guide.

Holding On to Faith in the Midst of Complexity

In a landscape filled with denominations, doctrines, and traditions, it's easy to feel pulled in different directions. But a strong, vibrant faith isn't anchored by uniformity—it's anchored by intimacy with God. We don't have to abandon religion altogether, but we do need to recognise when form has overtaken function.

There are three foundational ways to keep faith alive and growing, even amidst complexity:

1. **Focus on the Essentials**
   Strip it back. What does your faith really stand for? What core truths do you live by? Faith thrives when it's centred on love, humility, justice, mercy, and grace. These are not denominational ideals—they are Kingdom values. When we root ourselves in what matters most, we allow faith to breathe and speak freely, rather than being smothered by unnecessary weight.

2. **Cultivate a Personal Relationship with God**
   A personal walk with God is not optional—it's essential. No priest, pastor, or preacher can substitute your own communion with the Divine. Through prayer, stillness, scripture, worship, and honest conversation, you come to know God—not just know about Him. This intimacy becomes your compass, helping you to discern what is real from what is simply religious noise.

3. **Engage in Practices that Deepen Faith**
   Faith grows through practice. This could be through daily prayer, silence, acts of service, sacred reading, or time in nature.

Spiritual disciplines don't have to be complicated or prescribed—they simply need to be consistent. What matters is not the form they take, but the fruit they bear in your life: peace, joy, humility, wisdom, compassion.

These three anchors—essentials, intimacy, and practice—help us remain rooted in faith, even when religion feels confusing or heavy. They bring us back to what matters: not performance, but presence. Not ritual, but relationship.

4. **Saints Beyond Systems**

   Across history, many have chosen to live out their faith boldly, often beyond the limits of their religious context. Their lives remind us that faith isn't confined by robes, titles, or institutions—it is lived.

St. Francis of Assisi: Faith Made Simple

One of the clearest examples is St. Francis of Assisi. Born into privilege in 12th-century Italy, Francis walked away from wealth and prestige to embrace a life of radical simplicity, humility, and love. He didn't rebel against the Church, but neither did he conform to its comfort. His faith compelled him to serve the poor, embrace lepers, speak to nature, and live without possessions. His life became a living sermon—no pulpit required. He found God in birdsong, in hunger, in the eyes of beggars. And in doing so, he reminded the Church—and us—that faith has never been about buildings or robes or doctrines alone. It's about how we walk. How we love. How we live.

Martin Luther King Jr.'s Prophetic Voice

Another powerful example of faith expressed beyond religious boundaries is found in the life of Dr Martin Luther King Jr. Though deeply rooted in his Christian heritage as a Baptist minister, King's vision extended beyond denominational lines. His bold pursuit of justice, equality, and non-violent resistance was not only an expression of moral conviction, but a direct outworking of his faith. King's sermons, speeches, and writings reflected a deep commitment to God's justice. His faith did not remain confined to the pulpit—it took to the streets, the courts, and the hearts of a nation. By standing firm in the face of violence, resistance, and hate, King showed that living faith is not silent in the face of injustice. It speaks. It acts. It leads.

King's legacy reminds us that true faith will often challenge religious systems rather than hide within them. His life compels us to examine how our own beliefs show up in the public square, and whether we are using our faith to uphold justice or merely protect comfort.

5. The Dynamic Tension of Faith and Doubt

Faith and doubt are often misunderstood as opposites. In truth, they are companions on the journey. Faith is not certainty. It's not the absence of questions. Rather, faith is the courage to keep walking even when the path is unclear. It is the decision to trust in God's presence, even when we cannot trace His hand. Doubt arises from the raw complexities of life—from grief, confusion, suffering, and the aching silence of unanswered prayers. But doubt is not the enemy of faith. It is often the spark that ignites deeper seeking. As questions arise, so too can wisdom, compassion, and maturity. Doubt challenges the superficial and invites us into something more enduring— something real.

Faith chooses to believe when there is no proof. Doubt asks if the belief is worth holding. Together, they keep us honest. Embracing this paradox is part of spiritual growth. Faith that has never wrestled with doubt may be shallow. But faith that has journeyed through doubt—

and emerged still anchored—is often the kind that sustains us through storms.

This dynamic interplay does not mean we live in constant uncertainty. Rather, it means we are willing to hold mystery with reverence. It means we understand that wrestling is not a sign of weakness, but of engagement. We are not abandoned in our questioning; we are being refined.

A Faith That Lives and Breathes

Living out our faith in a world that sometimes feels cynical or rigid takes more than religious routine. It takes authenticity. It takes courage. It takes honesty about the questions we carry, and a willingness to keep trusting anyway. When we focus on what really matters—loving God, loving others, walking humbly, seeking justice, and living truthfully—we begin to move beyond empty religion and into a living faith. We're no longer checking boxes. We're living lives that radiate grace, mercy, and integrity. We are not called to perfection, but to presence. Not to performance, but to participation. And as we walk that out—sometimes in certainty, sometimes in silence—we bear witness to a God who meets us in both.

THE COMPLEX RELATIONSHIP BETWEEN FAITH AND RELIGION

Faith and religion are often spoken of in the same breath, yet they are not the same. Faith is personal. It's the lived experience of trust, devotion, and surrender to something greater than ourselves. Religion, by contrast, is the structure—the beliefs, practices, and institutions that give form to that inner faith (Stark & Bainbridge, 1985, p. 12). The two are related, but not interchangeable. One can have deep faith with little religion, or be deeply religious with little true faith.

The Double-Edged Nature of Religion

Religion can offer immense value. It provides community, shared meaning, and traditions that anchor and guide. As sociologist Émile Durkheim observed, religion binds people together through shared symbols and sacred practices (Durkheim, 1912, p. 47). It gives language to mystery and provides rituals for life's great thresholds—birth, death, love, loss.

But religion also has its shadow. When institutions prioritise rules over relationship, or when dogma becomes more important than love, religion can become a cage rather than a compass. As Paul Tillich warned, "Religion can be a prison, but it can also be a liberating force" (Tillich, 1957, p. 15). This paradox reminds us that while religion may lead us to God, it can also distract us from Him.

The Risks of Exclusivity and Dogmatism

Religious traditions, if held too tightly, can divide rather than unite. An exclusivist mindset—where only one path is deemed valid—can lead to intolerance, pride, and violence. When we no longer listen to others, when we assume our way is the only way, we shut the door to humility, growth, and compassion. Rigid doctrine can also stunt personal development. Faith was never meant to be static or shallow. But when questioning is discouraged, and complexity is reduced to formulas, people either conform or quietly disengage. They may show up, say the right words, even perform the rituals—yet inside, their faith has gone numb.

Most painfully, religion can obscure the very heart of spirituality: love, grace, kindness, and truth. When the rituals take centre stage and relationship takes a back seat, the soul begins to dry out. Jesus himself confronted this when he told the Pharisees, "You honour me with your lips, but your hearts are far from me" (Matthew 15:8). The danger is not just hypocrisy—it is hollowness.

Embracing the Paradox

To benefit from religion, we must engage it with both reverence and discernment. Religion can guide us—but it must not replace personal encounter. We are invited to look past the form and find the essence. To ask: does this lead me closer to God or further from Him? Does this nurture love or fear? Compassion or control? We must also learn to embrace difference. Not all who follow Christ will do so in the same way.

By making space for diverse expressions of faith, we honour the mystery and vastness of God. Spiritual maturity doesn't require uniformity—it requires humility. A deeper spirituality transcends performance and posturing. It asks for surrender, for truth, for connection with the heart of God. We may use religion to get there, but the journey itself is spiritual, personal, and unfolding.

Jesus and the Paradox of Faith and Religion

Nowhere is the paradox of Big Faith and Little Religion clearer than in the life of Jesus. On one hand, he championed the power of faith—faith as small as a mustard seed, yet capable of moving mountains (Matthew 17:20). On the other hand, he fiercely rebuked the religious elite for their empty rituals and legalistic posturing. "Woe to you," he said, "you whitewashed tombs... beautiful on the outside, but full of dead bones within" (Matthew 23:27). Jesus was not anti-religion, but he was never confined by it. His ministry redefined what it meant to be spiritual. It wasn't about ticking religious boxes—it was about healing the sick, welcoming the outsider, forgiving the sinner, and calling people to a living, breathing relationship with God.

What's remarkable is that Jesus never judged people based on how much faith they had—only on whether their hearts were open. To the Roman centurion, he said, "I have not found anyone in Israel with such great faith" (Matthew 8:10). And to his own disciples, trembling in the storm, he said gently, "You of little faith, why did you doubt?" (Matthew 14:31). Both were loved. Both were taught. Both were met with grace. As N.T. Wright reminds us, "Jesus' message was not about getting people to believe certain doctrines, but about calling people to follow him, to trust him, and to live under his lordship" (Wright, 2012). This was faith in action. A faith that walked, wept, touched, challenged, and transformed.

A Faith that Lives and Breathes

In the end, Jesus didn't measure people by their religion—he looked at their hearts. The woman who washed his feet with tears, the tax collector who repented, the thief on the cross—none of them had perfect theology. But they had faith. Raw, humble, surrendered faith. Henri Nouwen once said, "The spiritual life is not a life of perfection, but a life of surrender, a life of letting go, and a life of trust" (Nouwen, 1999). Jesus embodied this truth—and invites us into it. Big Faith doesn't mean loud faith. Little Religion doesn't mean no structure. It means we prioritise the living presence of God over the rituals that point to Him. We seek life, not just language. Surrender, not just systems.

Summary

Religion can be both a sacred guide and a stumbling block. It can help us find God—or cause us to miss Him. Jesus showed us how to live a faith that goes beyond performance—a faith rooted in trust, love, and transformation. As we embrace the paradox of Big Faith and Little Religion, may we learn to walk in a way that honours both truth and grace, knowing that real faith lives not in temples, but in hearts fully alive to God.

LIVING OUT FAITH IN A POST-RELIGIOUS WORLD

In today's world, many are turning away from traditional religious structures but not from the search for meaning. This so-called "post-religious" age is marked by a longing for spiritual depth that isn't confined to dogma, denomination, or institutional norms. People are seeking a more personal, authentic, and transformative expression of faith—one that speaks to their lived experience. As philosopher Charles Taylor observes, *"We live in a world where the old certainties are crumbling, and people are seeking new ways to express their spirituality"* (Taylor, 2007, p. 12) [1]. This doesn't mean faith is disappearing. Rather, it's shifting. Many still yearn for connection with something greater than themselves, even if they no longer find that connection through religion as they once knew it. Faith becomes something lived and felt—less about compliance with tradition, and more about alignment with truth.

The Complex Relationship Between Faith and Religion

Faith and religion often travel together, but they are not the same. Faith is personal. It is the internal compass that points us toward God, meaning, and trust in the unseen. Religion, by contrast, is the external structure—doctrines, rituals, institutions—that seeks to give faith a communal expression (Stark & Bainbridge, 1985, p. 12) [2]. One can exist without the other. Some have deep, vibrant faith with little religion. Others follow religious practice yet feel spiritually disconnected.

As theologian Paul Tillich reminds us, *"Religion can be a prison, but it can also be a liberating force"* (Tillich, 1957, p. 15) [3]. It can support and deepen faith—or obscure it. When religion is used to control, exclude, or shame, it does more harm than good. But when it points us to love, truth, and transformation, it becomes a wellspring of life.

Navigating the Complexities of Religious Traditions

Religious traditions carry weight—history, culture, beauty, and baggage. They can offer stability and community, but they can also become rigid and stifling. The challenge is to discern what nourishes faith and what hinders it. To maintain a strong and vibrant faith, we must return to the heart of what we believe. This means focusing not on rules or rituals, but on the core values that make faith alive—love, justice, mercy, humility, and grace. As Dietrich Bonhoeffer puts it, *"The essence of faith is not a set of propositions, but a personal relationship with God"* (Bonhoeffer, 1955, p. 15) [4]. This relationship is not mediated by tradition alone. It is deepened through honesty, prayer, service, community, and surrender. And it must remain open to mystery. As Søren Kierkegaard notes, *"Faith is a risk, a leap into the unknown"* (Kierkegaard, 1843, p. 15) [5]. True faith requires trust, not certainty.

Embracing the Paradox of Big Faith Little Religion

To embrace big faith and little religion is to live in tension. It is to honour the depth of spiritual conviction without becoming enslaved to religious conformity. It means being open to tradition—but not bound by it. It means pursuing truth—even when that truth moves beyond the walls of institutional religion. This approach doesn't reject religion outright—it reframes it. Religion becomes a tool, not a taskmaster. A gateway, not a gatekeeper. A path, not the point. Living this way requires courage. It means we may walk a path that looks different from those around us. But it also means we are more likely to experience a faith that is real, raw, and relevant. A faith that can breathe.

MAKING IT THROUGH WITH LITTLE FAITH AND LITTLE RELIGION – STORIES OF RESILIENCE

Life can be challenging, and there are times when our faith may be shaken—or when formal religion offers little comfort. Yet even in such seasons, people find remarkable ways to endure. This chapter shares stories of individuals who have faced overwhelming obstacles and still managed to uncover strength and resilience in the midst of uncertainty.

The Reality of Uncertainty and Doubt

Life is inherently unpredictable, and uncertainty is an inevitable part of the human experience. Even people of strong faith encounter periods of doubt, moments when their beliefs are tested, and their values feel fragile. As theologian Paul Tillich reminds us, *"Doubt is not the opposite of faith, but an element of faith"* (Tillich, 1957, p. 15) [1].

Stories of Resilience

Despite these challenges, many people have managed to cultivate resilience and preserve their sense of purpose. The stories in this chapter include those who have lived through illness, loss, trauma, and persecution—and yet, in their darkest hours, uncovered a flicker of hope. Sometimes their strength came from faith. Other times, it came from something less visible but no less powerful.

The Role of Faith in Resilience

Faith can provide a sense of meaning, purpose, and inner grounding during adversity. Psychologist Kenneth Pargament writes, *"Faith can be a powerful resource for coping with stress and trauma"* (Pargament, 1997, p. 12) [2]. Whether it's trust in God, belief in divine purpose, or simply hope for a better day, faith—however small—can serve as a life raft when everything else is crumbling.

The Importance of Community and Support

But resilience is rarely sustained in isolation. Community matters. A strong network of family, friends, or spiritual companions can make a profound difference. Sociologist Émile Durkheim observed, *"Religion is not just a personal matter, but a social one"* (Durkheim, 1912, p. 10) [3]. That shared connection—whether in a place of worship, a kitchen, or a hospital room—can offer the encouragement needed to carry on.

The Paradox of Little Faith and Great Miracles

What's striking is how often these stories reveal a paradox: that Little Faith can still open the door to Great Miracles. Some of the most transformative breakthroughs happen not in moments of strong, certain belief—but in seasons of near-defeat. These accounts challenge the idea that unwavering faith is required to experience God's intervention or healing. Sometimes, miracles meet us when we're barely hanging on.

Summary

Making it through life's hardest moments with little faith and little religion doesn't mean surviving empty-handed. It means holding on to what you can—community, hope, a mustard seed of trust—and discovering that even the smallest thread of belief can weave something beautiful. These stories remind us that faith, though fragile, still matters. And sometimes, that's enough.

MIRACLES – THE INTERSECTION OF FAITH AND REALITY

What are miracles, and how do they relate to our faith? This chapter explores the concept of miracles from both religious and humanistic perspectives, examining how faith shapes our understanding of the world and its many mysteries.

Defining Miracles

Miracles are events or experiences that transcend the ordinary and defy explanation by natural laws or principles. They can be understood as interruptions or interventions in the natural course of events, often attributed to a divine or supernatural force (Hume, 1748, p. 12) [1]. These moments may come in the form of healings, visions, prophetic dreams, or other extraordinary phenomena.

The Nature of Authentic Miracles

The idea of miracles has long fascinated and divided thinkers. Some remain sceptical of their validity, while others testify to life-changing experiences that defy logic or science. Authentic miracles are not simply rare or unusual events—they are characterised by a supernatural origin, the absence of human intervention, and a clear transcendence of natural laws.

When a miracle unfolds with no human interference, it seems as though reality itself is touched by a higher force. These experiences stretch our understanding of what is possible and open us to the possibility of something beyond our comprehension.

The Characteristics of Authentic Miracles

So what defines an authentic miracle?

1. Supernatural Origin – It cannot be explained by natural causes.

2. Absence of Human Intervention – There is no manipulation or human orchestration.

3. Transcendence of Natural Laws – The event clearly supersedes natural order.

This perspective resonates across spiritual and philosophical traditions, many of which interpret miracles as expressions of divine power, grace, or intention.

The Implications of Authentic Miracles

If miracles truly happen, their existence forces us to reconsider the nature of reality. They remind us that what we perceive and understand may not be the whole story. This opens the door to awe, wonder, and a renewed sense of spiritual curiosity. Recognising miracles as possible deepens our faith and invites us to remain humble before the mysteries of existence.

Religious Perspectives on Miracles

In many religious traditions, miracles are seen as divine interventions that validate a prophet's message or reveal God's character. In Christianity, miracles are viewed as signs of God's compassion and glory. Jesus' healing of the blind man, for instance, not only restored sight but also revealed the work of God in a broken world (John 9:1–38, KJV) [2]. When John the Baptist questioned Jesus' mission, Jesus pointed to miracles as evidence: *"The blind receive their sight, the lame walk, the lepers are cleansed..."* (Matthew 11:2–6, KJV) [3].

Humanistic Perspectives on Miracles

From a humanistic lens, miracles may not defy nature, but they certainly elevate the human spirit. They are understood as moments of unexpected transformation—stories of hope, survival, and inner change. As Norman Cousins puts it, these miracles can reflect *"the will to live and the body's extraordinary power to heal"* (Cousins, 1979, p. 12) [4]. They are less about divine intervention and more about the remarkable capacities of human resilience, compassion, and imagination.

The Intersection of Faith and Reality

Miracles live at the intersection of faith and reality. Our faith deeply affects how we interpret the extraordinary, and in turn, extraordinary experiences often shape and stretch our faith. As William James observed, *"Faith creates its own verification"* (James, 1902, p. 12) [5]. A person of faith might see divine purpose where others see coincidence. The miracle, then, is as much about perception as it is about event.

The Paradox of Miracles and Faith

This creates a paradox: miracles can strengthen faith, but sometimes faith is what allows us to perceive the miracle in the first place. Søren Kierkegaard framed this beautifully when he wrote, *"Faith is a risk, a leap into the unknown"* (Kierkegaard, 1843, p. 15) [6]. Faith opens our eyes to possibilities that logic might reject—and in doing so, helps us encounter the divine in unexpected places.

Summary

Miracles are not just moments that break the rules of nature—they are also invitations to explore the mysteries of faith, reality, and human experience. Whether viewed through a religious or humanistic lens, miracles inspire awe, renew faith, and remind us that there is still wonder to be found. They challenge our assumptions and expand our understanding of what's possible, reminding us that some truths are not easily explained—but deeply felt.

FAITH IS DAILY BREAD –

NOURISHING OUR SOULS

Faith is not a one-time event; it is a daily rhythm—a way of living that requires attention, care, and nourishment. This chapter explores how faith can be sustained and deepened, even in the midst of busy and demanding lives.

The Daily Practice of Faith

Faith is not static. It is a living force that needs daily tending. Jesus, when tempted in the wilderness, declared, *"Man shall not live by bread alone, but by every word that proceeds out of the mouth of God"* (Matthew 4:4, KJV) [1]. Just as our bodies need food, our souls require nourishment—through God's presence, promises, and truth.

Cultivating Faith through Spiritual Practices

Faith is strengthened through intentional habits that create space for the divine. Practices like prayer, stillness, worship, and scripture reading allow us to listen, reflect, and reset. Richard Foster puts it this way: *"Spiritual practices are the means by which we experience the presence of God in our lives"* (Foster, 1998, p. 12) [2]. These small, quiet acts of devotion become sacred anchors for a deeper, more resilient faith.

The Importance of Community and Accountability

We were never meant to walk this journey alone. Community provides spiritual support, loving correction, and shared encouragement. As Dietrich Bonhoeffer reminds us, *"The church is the community of those who are called to faith"* (Bonhoeffer, 1955, p. 15) [3]. When we show up for one another in worship, conversation, or prayer, we keep one another grounded in the faith we proclaim.

Navigating the Challenges of Busy and Chaotic Lives

In the rush of modern life, it can feel impossible to slow down for spiritual practice. But it is often in those very moments—when things feel overwhelming—that faith becomes a lifeline. *"I can do all things through Christ who strengthens me"* (Philippians 4:13, KJV) [4]. This is not a promise of ease, but of sustaining grace. Faith is not about escape from difficulty—it is what equips us to face it.

The Role of Faith in Promoting Resilience and Well-being

Beyond spiritual enrichment, faith has tangible benefits. Research consistently shows that faith can improve mental health, reduce anxiety, and foster resilience. As Harold Koenig observes, *"Faith is a powerful resource for promoting health and well-being"* (Koenig, 2015, p. 12) [5]. Whether in quiet confidence or desperate prayer, faith gives us strength when human strength falls short.

Summary

Faith is not a single event, but a daily act of remembering, trusting, and returning. It grows through spiritual practices, flourishes in community, and sustains us in hardship. Like bread for the body, faith feeds the soul. It grounds us in what is eternal and carries us through what is not.

CONCLUSION:

RECLAIMING THE SACRED

BEYOND THE SYSTEM

What if faith wasn't something to perform, but something to live? What if God could meet you, not through perfection or pressure, but in the mess, the wonder, and the questions?

Big Faith Little Religion, Little Faith Great Miracles has been a journey—an honest search for something deeper than inherited belief and more spacious than institutional rules. It has been about unlearning what no longer brings life, and leaning into a faith that can stretch, breathe, and grow with you.

This is not about throwing faith away. It's about finding it again—beneath the layers, beyond the fear, outside the lines. It's about choosing presence over performance. Love over fear. Trust over control.

Whether you've been deconstructing, rebuilding, or simply wondering if there's more—this book has walked beside you as a quiet companion. Not with rigid answers, but with open hands and an open heart.

Because real faith doesn't demand certainty. It invites connection. It welcomes doubt. It makes space for mystery.

And perhaps most of all, it reminds us that the sacred is not locked inside a system—it's alive within us, calling us back to what is true, what is kind, and what is real.

So may your faith be lived, not imposed. May it move with you, grow through you, and meet you exactly where you are.

And may it always, always breathe.

ABOUT THE AUTHOR

Godwin Booysen is a pragmatic Military Chaplain, renowned Specialist Wellness Counsellor, and Advanced Religious Specialist in Christian Pastoral Counselling. He empowers individuals and communities with compassion, empathy, and leadership, skillfully navigating complex emergency situations and providing guidance and support to those coping with traumatic events & environments. His passion for empowering others drives him to continue growing and learning, ensuring that his clients receive the best possible support.

Godwin has worked closely with vulnerable populations, providing support and guidance. He has had the privilege of serving in various military units and a church ministry running parallel to it for ten years, officiating weddings, speaking at graduations, and providing comfort to widows and families of fallen soldiers.

Godwin's life's journey has been marked by significant personal growth and evolution over the past three decades, alongside numerous accomplishments. This transformative process has not only been incredibly fulfilling but has also profoundly deepened his understanding of faith and spirituality.

Dr. Heywars B. Ewart III, a renowned Christian psychotherapist, aptly describes Godwin's work: "A key factor in making Godwin special, besides outstanding scholarship, is that he has demonstrated a keen understanding of distressed people and an ability to arrive at the core issues quickly. He has minimized the suffering of many souls. In addition, he holds an intrinsic capacity to blend theology and psychology, a quality which is quite rare in my 34 years of experience."

Godwin's calm and composed demeanor, paired with a steadfast commitment to confidentiality, earns him the respect and admiration of his peers. His unique blend of compassion, empathy, and leadership makes him an exceptional servant of all those he encounters.

REFERENCES

Part 1

Chapter 1

[1] Tagore, R. (1912). *Gitanjali*. Macmillan.

[2] Tillich, P. (1957). *Dynamics of Faith*. Harper & Row.

[3] Chopra, D. (2000). *The Spontaneous Fulfillment of Desire*. Harmony Books.

[4] Rilke, R. M. (1929). *Letters to a Young Poet*. W.W. Norton & Company.

[5] Chopra, D. (2000). *The Spontaneous Fulfillment of Desire*. Harmony Books.

[6] Merton, T. (1979). *No Man Is an Island*. Harcourt.

[7] Chopra, D. (2000). *The Spontaneous Fulfillment of Desire*. Harmony Books.

[8] James, W. (1902). *The Varieties of Religious Experience*. Longmans, Green & Co.

[9] Jung, C. G. (1964). *Man and His Symbols*. Dell Publishing.

[10] Tillich, P. (1957). *Dynamics of Faith*. Harper & Row.

[11] Brown, B. (2010). *The Gifts of Imperfection*. Hazelden Publishing.

[12] Tolle, E. (1997). *The Power of Now: A Guide to Spiritual Enlightenment*. Namaste Publishing.

[13] Feynman, R. P. (1965). *The Character of Physical Law*. BBC Publications.

[14] Plato. (c. 380 BCE). *The Apology*.

[15] Dass, R. (1971). *Be Here Now*. Lama Foundation.

[1] Rohr, R. (2009). *Faith and Doubt*. St. Anthony Messenger Press.

[2] Rogers, C. R. (1961). *On Becoming a Person: A Therapist's View of Psychotherapy*. Houghton Mifflin.

[3] Merton, T. (1967). *Conjectures of a Guilty Bystander*. Doubleday.

Chapter 2

[1] Tillich, P. (1957). Dynamics of Faith. Harper & Row.

[2] Chopra, D. (2000). The Spontaneous Fulfillment of Desire: Harnessing the Infinite Power of Coincidence. Harmony Books.

[3] Dalai Lama (1999). The Art of Happiness: A Handbook for Living. Riverhead Books.

[4] Jung, C. G. (1964). Man and His Symbols. Dell Publishing.

[5] Doug Murren (1999). Churches That Heal: Becoming a Church That Mends Broken Hearts and Restores Shattered Lives. Howard Publishing Company.

[1] Merton, T. (1961). *New Seeds of Contemplation*. New Directions Publishing.

[2] Maslow, A. H. (1962). Toward a Psychology of Being. Harper & Row.

[3] Buechner, F. (1992). *Listening to Your Life: Daily Meditations with Frederick Buechner*. HarperOne.

[4] Dalai Lama. (1999). *Ethics for the New Millennium*. Riverhead Books.

[5] Tolle, E. (2003). *Stillness Speaks*. New World Library.

[1] Nouwen, H. J. M. (1975). *Reaching Out: The Three Movements of the Spiritual Life*. Doubleday.
[2] Jung, C. G. (1964). *Man and His Symbols*. Doubleday.
[3] Chopra, D. (2000). *How to Know God: The Soul's Journey into the Mystery of Mysteries*. Harmony Books.

[1] Tillich, P. (1957). Dynamics of Faith. Harper & Row.

[2] Chopra, D. (2000). The Spontaneous Fulfillment of Desire. Harmony Books.

[3] Jung, C. G. (1964). Man and His Symbols. Dell Publishing.

[4] Palmer, P. J. (2004). A Hidden Wholeness: The Journey Toward an Undivided Life. Jossey-Bass.

[5] Armstrong, K. (2009). The Case for God. Alfred A. Knopf.

[6] Nouwen, H. J. M. (1983). *Compassion: A Reflection on the Christian Life*. Image Books.

[7] Brown, B. (2010). *The Gifts of Imperfection: Let Go of Who You Think You're Supposed to Be and Embrace Who You Are*. Hazelden Publishing.

[8] Kierkegaard, S. (1843). Fear and Trembling. Penguin Books.

[9] Nouwen, H. J. M. (1986). *Reaching Out: The Three Movements of the Spiritual Life*. Image Books.

[1] Jung, C. G. (1964). Man and His Symbols. Dell Publishing.

[2] Tolle, E. (1997). The Power of Now. Namaste Publishing.

[3] Frankl, V. E. (1946). Man's Search for Meaning. Beacon Press.

[4] Rogers, C. R. (1961). On Becoming a Person. Houghton Mifflin.

[5] Palmer, P. J. (2004). A Hidden Wholeness: The Journey Toward an Undivided Life. Jossey-Bass.

Chapter 3

[1] Fromm, E. (1950). *Psychoanalysis and Religion*. New Haven, CT: Yale University Press.

[2] Armstrong, K. (2009). *The Case for God*. London: The Bodley Head.

[3] Maslow, A. H. (1962). *Toward a Psychology of Being*. Princeton, NJ: Van Nostrand.

[4] Jung, C. G. (1964). *Man and His Symbols*. London: Aldus Books.

[5] Palmer, P. J. (2004). *A Hidden Wholeness: The Journey Toward an Undivided Life*. San Francisco: Jossey-Bass.

[6] Frankl, V. E. (1946). *Man's Search for Meaning*. Boston: Beacon Press.

[7] Watts, A. (1951). *The Wisdom of Insecurity: A Message for an Age of Anxiety*. New York: Pantheon Books.

[8] Tillich, P. (1957). *The Courage to Be*. New Haven, CT: Yale University Press.

[9] Chopra, D. (2000). *How to Know God: The Soul's Journey into the Mystery of Mysteries*. New York: Harmony Books.

Chapter 4

[1] Fromm, E. (1950). *The Authoritarian Personality*. New York: Harper & Row.

[2] Maslow, A. H. (1962). *Toward a Psychology of Being*. Princeton, NJ: Van Nostrand.

[3] Langone, M. D. (2000). *Recovery from Cults: Help for Victims of Psychological and Spiritual Abuse*. New York: W. W. Norton & Company.

[4] Armstrong, K. (2009). *The Case for God*. London: The Bodley Head.

[5] Palmer, P. J. (2004). *A Hidden Wholeness: The Journey Toward an Undivided Life*. San Francisco: Jossey-Bass.

[6] Chopra, D. (2000). *How to Know God: The Soul's Journey into the Mystery of Mysteries*. New York: Harmony Books.

[7] Wilber, K. (1996). *A Brief History of Everything*. Boston: Shambhala Publications.

[8] Tillich, P. (1957). *The Courage to Be*. New Haven: Yale University Press.

[9] Kierkegaard, S. (1843). *Fear and Trembling*. (Translated edition varies; often cited from Princeton University Press or Penguin Classics).

Chapter 5

[1] Gladwell, M. (2000). *The Tipping Point: How Little Things Can Make a Big Difference*. Little, Brown.

[2] Bandura, A. (1997). *Self-Efficacy: The Exercise of Control*. W.H. Freeman.

[3] Collins, J. (2001). *Good to Great: Why Some Companies Make the Leap... and Others Don't*. HarperBusiness.

[4] Hardy, D. (2010). *The Compound Effect: Jumpstart Your Income, Your Life, Your Success*. Vanguard Press.

[5] Duhigg, C. (2012). *The Power of Habit: Why We Do What We Do in Life and Business*. Random House.

[6] Amabile, T. M. (1988). *The Progress Principle: Using Small Wins to Ignite Joy, Engagement, and Creativity at Work*. Harvard Business Review Press.

[7] Palmer, P. J. (2004). *A Hidden Wholeness: The Journey Toward an Undivided Life*. Jossey-Bass.

[8] Chopra, D. (2000). *How to Know God: The Soul's Journey into the Mystery of Mysteries*. Harmony Books.

[9] Tillich, P. (1957). *Dynamics of Faith*. Harper & Row.

[10] Cohen, S. (2004). *Social Relationships and Health*. American Psychologist, 59(8), 676–684.

[11] Frankl, V. E. (1946). *Man's Search for Meaning*. Beacon Press.

[12] Duckworth, A. (2016). *Grit: The Power of Passion and Perseverance*. Scribner.

[13] Dweck, C. S. (2006). *Mindset: The New Psychology of Success.* Random House.

Chapter 6

[1] Kelman, H. C. (1961). Processes of opinion change. *Public Opinion Quarterly*, 25(1), 57–78.

[2] Branch, T. (1988). *Parting the Waters: America in the King Years 1954–63.* New York: Simon & Schuster.

[3] Maxwell, J. C. (2005). *The 360° Leader: Developing Your Influence from Anywhere in the Organization.* Nashville: Thomas Nelson.

[4] Bandura, A. (1997). *Self-Efficacy: The Exercise of Control.* New York: W. H. Freeman.

[5] Kane, K. (2013). *Little Sisters of the Poor: The Journey of Faith and Service.* Catholic Press.

[6] Florida, R. (2002). *The Rise of the Creative Class: And How It's Transforming Work, Leisure, Community and Everyday Life.* New York: Basic Books.

[7] Kotter, J. P. (1996). *Leading Change.* Boston: Harvard Business School Press.

[8] Denning, S. (2005). *The Leader's Guide to Storytelling: Mastering the Art and Discipline of Business Narrative.* San Francisco: Jossey-Bass.

[9] Kotler, P. (2002). *Marketing Moves: A New Approach to Profits, Growth and Renewal.* Boston: Harvard Business School Press.

[1] Bandura, A. (1997). Self-efficacy: The exercise of control. New York: Freeman.

[2] Cialdini, R. B. (2009). Influence: Science and practice (5th ed.). Boston: Allyn & Bacon.

[3] Florida, R. (2002). The rise of the creative class: And how it's transforming work, leisure, community and everyday life. New York: Basic Books.

[4] Locke, E. A., & Latham, G. P. (2002). Building a practically useful theory of goal setting. American Psychologist, 57(9), 701-710.

[5] Cohen, S. (2004). Social relationships and mortality: An analysis of the National Longitudinal Study of Adolescent Health. Journal of Behavioural Medicine, 27(5), 401-415.

[6] Senge, P. M. (1990). The fifth discipline: The art & practice of the learning organization. New York: Doubleday.

Chapter 7

[1] Fromm, E. (1950). *Psychoanalysis and Religion*. New Haven: Yale University Press.
[2] Maslow, A. H. (1962). *Toward a Psychology of Being*. Princeton, NJ: Van Nostrand.
[3] Maslow, A. H. (1962). *Toward a Psychology of Being*. Princeton, NJ: Van Nostrand.
[4] Tillich, P. (1957). *The Protestant Era*. Chicago: University of Chicago Press.
[5] Palmer, P. (2004). *A Hidden Wholeness: The Journey Toward an Undivided Life*. San Francisco: Jossey-Bass.
[6] Chopra, D. (2000). *The Seven Spiritual Laws of Success: A Practical*

Guide to the Fulfillment of Your Dreams. San Rafael, CA: Amber-Allen Publishing.

[7] Rokeach, M. (1973). *The Nature of Human Values*. New York: Free Press.

[8] Kierkegaard, S. (1843). *Either/Or: A Fragment of Life*. Translated by David F. Swenson and Lillian Marvin Swenson (1944). Princeton, NJ: Princeton University Press.

[9] Francis de Sales. (1609). *Introduction to the Devout Life*. Translated by John K. Ryan (1950). New York: Image Books.

Chapter 8

[1] Kanter, R. M. (2006). *Confidence: How Winning Streaks and Losing Streaks Begin and End*. New York: Crown Business.

[2] Duhigg, C. (2012). *The Power of Habit: Why We Do What We Do in Life and Business*. New York: Random House.

[3] Eliot, G. (1871). *Middlemarch: A Study of Provincial Life*. London: William Blackwood and Sons.

[4] Whitehead, A. N. (1926). *Religion in the Making*. Cambridge: Cambridge University Press.

[5] Parks, R. (1992). *Rosa Parks: My Story*. New York: Dial Books.

[6] Sharma, R. (2003). *The Saint, the Surfer, and the CEO: A Remarkable Story about Living Your Heart's Desires*. San Francisco: Hay House.

[7] Armstrong, K. (2009). *The Case for God*. London: The Bodley Head.

[8] Lee, N. R. (2001). *Social Marketing: Influencing Behaviors for Good.* Thousand Oaks: SAGE Publications.

[9] Küng, H. (1974). *Does God Exist? An Answer for Today.* London: Collins.

Chapter 9

[1] Emmons, R. A. (2003). *Thanks! How the New Science of Gratitude Can Make You Happier.* Houghton Mifflin.

[2] Kabat-Zinn, J. (2003). *Mindfulness for Beginners: Reclaiming the Present Moment—and Your Life.* Sounds True.

[3] Wrzesniewski, A., McCauley, C., Rozin, P., & Schwartz, B. (1997). Jobs, Careers, and Callings: People's Relations to Their Work. *Journal of Research in Personality*, 31(1), 21–33.

[4] Brown, B. (2010). *The Gifts of Imperfection: Let Go of Who You Think You're Supposed to Be and Embrace Who You Are.* Hazelden Publishing.

[5] Seligman, M. E. P. (2011). *Flourish: A Visionary New Understanding of Happiness and Well-being.* Free Press.

[6] Brown, B. (2012). *Daring Greatly: How the Courage to Be Vulnerable Transforms the Way We Live, Love, Parent, and Lead.* Gotham Books.

[7] Maxwell, J. C. (2006). *Today Matters: 12 Daily Practices to Guarantee Tomorrow's Success.* Center Street.

[8] Vanier, J. (1998). *Becoming Human.* Paulist Press.

[9] Neff, K. (2011). *Self-Compassion: The Proven Power of Being Kind to Yourself.* William Morrow.

[10] Coutu, D. (2002). How Resilience Works. *Harvard Business Review,* 80(5), 46–55.

[11] Nouwen, H. J. M. (1994). *The Inner Voice of Love: A Journey Through Anguish to Freedom.* Doubleday.

[12] Duckworth, A. (2016). *Grit: The Power of Passion and Perseverance.* Scribner.

[13] Beattie, M. (1990). *The Language of Letting Go: Daily Meditations for Codependents.* Hazelden Publishing.

[14] Enright, R. D. (2001). *Forgiveness Is a Choice: A Step-by-Step Process for Resolving Anger and Restoring Hope.* APA LifeTools.

[15] Lamott, A. (2006). *Plan B: Further Thoughts on Faith.* Riverhead Books.

Chapter 10

[1] Gilbert, E. (2009). *Eat, Pray, Love.* New York: Penguin.

[2] Clear, J. (2018). *Atomic Habits: An Easy & Proven Way to Build Good Habits & Break Bad Ones.* New York: Avery.

[3] Jeffers, S. (1987). *Feel the Fear and Do It Anyway.* New York: Ballantine Books.

[4] Covey, S. R. (1989). *The 7 Habits of Highly Effective People.* New York: Free Press.

[5] Williamson, M. (1992). *A Return to Love: Reflections on the Principles of A Course in Miracles.* New York: HarperOne.

[6] Godin, S. (2008). *Tribes: We Need You to Lead Us*. New York: Portfolio.

[7] Duckworth, A. (2016). *Grit: The Power of Passion and Perseverance*. New York: Scribner.

[8] Rohn, J. (2004). *The Five Major Pieces to the Life Puzzle*. Jim Rohn International.

[9] Goleman, D. (1995). *Emotional Intelligence: Why It Can Matter More Than IQ*. New York: Bantam Books.

[10] Collins, J. (2001). *Good to Great: Why Some Companies Make the Leap... and Others Don't*. New York: HarperBusiness.

[11] Achor, S. (2010). *The Happiness Advantage: The Seven Principles of Positive Psychology That Fuel Success and Performance at Work*. New York: Crown Business.

[12] Gilbert, E. (2015). *Big Magic: Creative Living Beyond Fear*. New York: Riverhead Books.

[13] Bandura, A. (1997). *Self-Efficacy: The Exercise of Control*. New York: W.H. Freeman.

[14] Tillich, P. (1957). *The Courage to Be*. New Haven: Yale University Press.

[15] Goleman, D. (1995). *Emotional Intelligence: Why It Can Matter More Than IQ*. New York: Bantam Books.

Part II

Camus, A. (1955). Return to Tipasa. Alfred A. Knopf.

Sartre, J. (1943). Being and Nothingness. Routledge.

Kierkegaard, S. (1843). Fear and Trembling. Penguin Books.

Tillich, P. (1957). Dynamics of Faith. Harper & Row.

Camus, A. (1942). The Myth of Sisyphus. Vintage Books.

Heidegger, M. (1927). Being and Time. State University of New York Press.

Hobbes, T. (1651). Leviathan. Oxford University Press.

Hume, D. (1748). An Enquiry Concerning Human Understanding. Oxford University Press.

Kane, R. (1996). The Significance of Free Will. Oxford University Press.

Sartre, J. (1943). Being and Nothingness. Routledge.

Spinoza, B. (1677). Ethics. Penguin Books.

Strawson, P. (1962). Freedom and Resentment. Proceedings of the British Academy.

Hardin, C. (1982). The Ethics of Free Will. Oxford University Press.

[1] Roets, E. (2022). *Statement by Deputy CEO of AfriForum in response to US asylum offer for White Afrikaners.* [Interview/Press Release].

[2] Mandela, N. (1993). *Long Walk to Freedom: The Autobiography of Nelson Mandela.* Boston: Little, Brown and Company.

[3] Roets, E. (2022). *Statement by Deputy CEO of AfriForum regarding cultural preservation and asylum offers.* [Interview/Press Release].

[1] Maslow, A. H. (1943). A theory of human motivation. Psychological Review, 50(4), 370-396.

[2] Bandura, A. (1997). Self-efficacy: The exercise of control. New York: Freeman.

[3] Holt-Lunstad, J., Smith, T. B., Baker, M., Harris, T., & Stephenson, D. (2015). *Loneliness and social isolation as risk factors for mortality: A meta-analytic review.* Perspectives on Psychological Science, 10(2), 227–237.

[4] Seligman, M. E. P. (2011). *Flourish: A Visionary New Understanding of Happiness and Well-being.* New York: Free Press.

Matthew Henry – *Matthew Henry's Commentary on the Whole Bible*

John Calvin – *Calvin's Commentaries*, particularly:
- Commentary on Genesis
- Commentary on Exodus
- Commentary on Job

Matthew 21:22 (NIV): "If you believe, you will receive whatever you ask for in prayer."

Romans 10:17 (NIV): "Consequently, faith comes from hearing the message, and the message is heard through the word about Christ."

1 Thessalonians 5:18 (NIV): "Give thanks in all circumstances; for this is God's will for you in Christ Jesus."

Psalm 51:17 (NIV): "My sacrifice, O God, is a broken spirit; a broken and contrite heart you, God, will not despise."

Philippians 4:8 (NIV): "Finally, brothers and sisters, whatever is true, whatever is noble, whatever is right, whatever is pure, whatever is lovely, whatever is admirable—if anything is excellent or praiseworthy—think about such things."

Part III

[1] James, W. (1902). The Varieties of Religious Experience. Longmans, Green, and Co.

[2] Tillich, P. (1957). Dynamics of Faith. Harper & Row.

[3] Matthew 17:20

[4] Hebrews 11:1 King James Version (KJV)

[5] Kierkegaard, S. (1843). Fear and Trembling. Penguin Books.

[6] Aquinas, T. (1274). Summa Theologica.

[7] Kant, I. (1781). Critique of Pure Reason.

[1] Berger, P. (1967). The Sacred Canopy: Elements of a Sociological Theory of Religion. Doubleday.

[2] Berry, T. (1973). The Dream of the Earth. Sierra Club Books.

[3] Durkheim, E. (1912). The Elementary Forms of the Religious Life. Oxford University Press.

[4] Merton, T.(1948) The Seven Story Mountain

Frankl, V. (1946). Man's Search for Meaning. Beacon Press.

[1] Hick, J. (1973). God and the Universe of Faiths. St. Martin's Press.

[2] Underhill, E. (1911). Mysticism: A Study in the Nature and Development of Spiritual Consciousness. Methuen.

[3] Frankl, V. (1946). Man's Search for Meaning. Beacon Press.

[4] Durkheim, E. (1912). The Elementary Forms of the Religious Life. Oxford University Press.

[5] Berger, P. (1967). The Sacred Canopy: Elements of a Sociological Theory of Religion. Doublday.

[6] Merton, T. (1948). The Seven Storey Mountain. Harcourt, Brace and Company.

[7] Berry, T. (1973). The Dream of the Earth. Sierra Club Books.

Genesis 12:1-9, King James Version (KJV).

James 2:26, King James Version (KJV).

John 9:1-38, King James Version (KJV).

Luke 10:25-37, King James Version (KJV).

James 2:26

Proverbs 3:5

Romans 10:1

[1] James 2:26, King James Version (KJV).

[2] Bonhoeffer, D. (1955). Ethics. SCM Press.

[3] Barth, K. (1936).The Church and The Churches.Wm. B

[4] Luther, M. (1520). The Babylonian Captivity of the Church.

[5] Catechism of the Catholic Church. (1992). Libreria Editrice Vaticana.

[6] McGrath, A. (2005). The Christian Theology Reader. Wiley-Blackwell.

[7] Wright, N.T. (2009). Justification: God's Plan & Paul's Vision. SPCK.

[1] Matthew 5:16, King James Version (KJV).

[2] James 2:26, King James Version (KJV).

[3] Wright, N.T. (2009). Justification: God's Plan & Paul's Vision. SPCK.

[1] Barth, K. (1936). Church Dogmatics. T&T Clark.

[2] James 2:26, King James Version (KJV).

[3] Bonhoeffer, D. (1955). The Cost of Discipleship. SCM Press.

[4] Matthew 5:16, King James Version (KJV).

[1] Tillich, P. (1957). Dynamics of Faith. Harper & Row.
[2] Mark 2:27, King James Version (KJV).

[1] Wright, N.T. (2012). Simply Jesus: A New Vision of Who He Was, What He Did, and Why He Matters. HarperOne.

[2] Nouwen, H. (1999). The Inner Voice of Love: A Journey Through Anguish to Freedom. Doubleday.

[1] Taylor, C. (2007). *A Secular Age*. Harvard University Press.

[2] Stark, R., & Bainbridge, W. S. (1985). *The Future of Religion: Secularization, Revival and Cult Formation*. University of California Press.

[3] Tillich, P. (1957). *Dynamics of Faith*. Harper & Row.

[4] Bonhoeffer, D. (1955). *The Cost of Discipleship*. SCM Press.

[5] Kierkegaard, S. (1843). *Fear and Trembling*. Penguin Classics (2003 edition).

1. Tillich, P. (1957). *Dynamics of Faith*. Harper & Row.

2. Pargament, K. (1997). *The Psychology of Religion and Coping*. Guilford Press.

3. Durkheim, É. (1912). *The Elementary Forms of the Religious Life*. Oxford University Press

1. Hume, D. (1748). *An Enquiry Concerning Human Understanding*. Oxford University Press.

2. John 9:1–38, King James Version (KJV).

3. Matthew 11:2–6, King James Version (KJV).

4. Cousins, N. (1979). *Anatomy of an Illness as Perceived by the Patient*. W.W. Norton & Company.

5. James, W. (1902). *The Varieties of Religious Experience*. Longmans, Green, and Co.

6. Kierkegaard, S. (1843). *Fear and Trembling*. Penguin Books.

1. Matthew 4:4, King James Version (KJV).

2. Foster, R. (1998). *Celebration of Discipline: The Path to Spiritual Growth*. HarperOne.

3. Bonhoeffer, D. (1955). *The Cost of Discipleship*. SCM Press.

4. Philippians 4:13, King James Version (KJV).

5. Koenig, H. (2015). *The Healing Power of Faith*. Templeton Press.

www.ingramcontent.com/pod-product-compliance
Lightning Source LLC
Chambersburg PA
CBHW021138090426
42740CB00008B/831